Not Alcoholic, But...

Will Piper

Published by Durbon Press
40 Mall Chambers
Kensington Mall
London W8 4DZ

Copyright © 2016 Will Piper

Author's website
www.notalcoholicbut.com

All rights reserved

Will Piper has asserted his right
under the Copyright, Designs and Patents Act 1988
to be identified as the author of this work

ISBN 978-1-53913-405-3

Also available as a Kindle ebook
ISBN 978-1-84396-428-5

**A CIP catalogue record for this
book is available from the British Library.**

Pre-press production
eBook Versions
27 Old Gloucester Street
London WC1N 3AX
www.ebookversions.com

Not Alcoholic, But...

Will Piper

Durbon Press

CONTENTS

Preface   **1**

Chapter One
Welcome to My Drinking World   **3**
My Drinking – An Introduction   **5**
When It All Started   **8**
University   **20**
Working For A Living   **26**
Middle-Aged, Middle-Class Drinker   **31**
Drinking Alone   **39**
Secret Drinking   **44**
The Bits I Tried To Forget   **50**

Chapter Two
My Last Year of Drinking   **65**

Chapter Three
Stopping Drinking –
Day One: The Day After
My Final Night of Drinking 89
Day Two: My First AA Meeting 94
Days 3 to 7 97
First Month 98
How Did I Get
Through Social Events? 100
Have I Stopped Wanting
to See My Friends? 104
Have They Stopped Wanting
to See Me? 104
How Does it Feel Looking
at Other People Drinking? 105
Christmas and Other
Big Festivals – Glastonbury! 108
Airports... and Holidays 111
Airports... and Holidays: One Year In 112
What Does A Bad Day Feel Like Now? 116
Highs and Lows 117
Financial Consequences 121
What Does My Future Hold? 122
What Lessons Can Be Learned
From My Own Experience? 123

Chapter Four
   Am I An Alcoholic? **125**

Chapter Five
   Desire – and the Resistance to Change **132**

Appendix **127**
   Measuring Your Relationship
   with Alcohol **137**
   Example 1 **138**
   Example 2 **139**
   Example 3 **139**

PREFACE

Drinkers come in all varieties, from homeless drunks to celebratory sippers. There are heavy drinkers who drink openly among family and friends, and those who prefer to hide their drinking from everyone around.

There are drinkers whose lives are ruled by alcohol, who need it at all social occasions. They rub shoulders at the same functions with drinkers who are as happy with orange juice as they are with wine.

Some exert self-control over their drinking and keep within imposed limits – either their own or their partners'. Others drink to black out every time.

I have met many people who don't drink for several weeks, then have a few and go off the rails. Others drink regularly and never get into difficulty.

Not Alcoholic, But… is for all these drinkers, but most especially the ones who, from time to time, worry that they might have a problem with alcohol.

CHAPTER ONE

Welcome to My Drinking World

I never really intended to stop drinking. What happened to my thirst was something of a mystery. I don't know whether I changed my desire or it changed me, but after 36 years of relatively trouble-free drinking, I quit.

You read many a tale about alcoholics drinking themselves into near oblivion before turning their lives around to fame and fortune. Well, this book isn't one of those stories.

What I want to do is explore my sudden change of desire in order to see if there are any lessons that could possibly be learned from it. This book is for heavy drinkers who are ambivalent about the excessiveness of their drinking and it is for those who haven't made up their mind whether they have a problem or what they will do about it if they do.

During my 36 years of drinking, the latter end particularly, I would occasionally worry about my consumption. It was usually on account of my behaviour after a bad incident – a drunken row, or making a fool of myself. Sometimes, it was about health or money.

In the aftermath of these incidents, I might read about the subject of alcohol on the internet or in books, and I would always find the same unsatisfactory information about the different types of alcoholics, about the Government guidelines for safe drinking, and a host of literature that was clearly aimed at drinkers who had resolved to give up.

There was nothing in between. And that's where I felt I was – in between.

So, this book is for drinkers who don't feel they are as bad as the worst out there for whatever reason, but on the other hand, feel like they should be getting a better handle on their own drinking (whatever that really means).

What I want to communicate to all such indecisive worriers is: don't fixate solely on how many units you think you can get away with drinking, or trying to analyse whether you might be an alcoholic, or whether you need to cut down your drinking, or indeed give it up altogether. What you should be questioning is your relationship with alcohol.

That's what this book aims to help with. At the end of this tale, I offer the reader a more useful set of questions to explore their own relationship with alcohol to see if their desire for it really is as strong as they think it is now.

What the reader chooses to do after that is entirely up to them. Even if they choose to carry on as before, this book will always be there for them in the future to test their desire and see if they are at last ready for something completely different.

But first I want to tell you a bit about my own relationship with alcohol.

My Drinking – An Introduction

I love that famous old quote of Vivian Stanshall's: "If I had all the money I spent on drink, I'd spend it on…drink." I love his brazen honesty, and I love that line because it summed me up. It encapsulated how I wanted to be seen by my friends and even colleagues.

On the one hand, it was just plain funny, and I wanted to be thought of as a funny drinker, an amusing drunk. It also told you how proud I was to be a heavy drinker, how it defined me. How rebellious I was. And in a breath, it conveyed where all my money had gone and where it would always go. And I was okay with that.

If you asked my friends what they thought of my

drinking, they would tell you that I was a good drunk by and large. That I came to life, that I made people laugh. It's what I wanted to hear, and they would have supported me in that view of myself. I'm sure they would. I liked to enjoy a night out, and I wanted everyone else to enjoy it too. Alcohol was the glue that held us together. I loved the way it could both crank everything up to a state of excitement and slow everything down, holding me, holding us in the moment like a photograph. I loved its soaring highs and that sense of adventure it gave.

I loved the way it allowed me to hit the slow-motion button in real time, so I could savour any moment however big or small – celebrating anything from a minor achievement at work to a victory in the cup, thunderous music booming all around me. Nothing adds pathos, euphoria, and tragedy to a situation like alcohol can. Its chaos is exciting and unpredictable. I loved drinking, and I was certain I was never going to stop loving it.

I'm sure there was a big dose of insecurity in there somewhere, but so what? Insecurity can be quite endearing, and I wanted to endear myself to those around me. And I was having a good time in the process. Alcohol ensured this, more or less, in all circumstances.

Alcohol had a sort of rollercoaster effect on my social life, creating big, surging highs followed by inevitable lows. You know, that terrible Sunday night feeling of finality when the party is over. But I always felt this was the natural way of things: the rough with the smooth.

Those big highs were well worth living for: Sunday drinking marathons; Friday pub and curry nights; sessions at the bar in airport lounges before flying off to the sun; festivals of never-ending music and cider; gin and tonics after work, wine with dinner, champagne to celebrate, whisky in coffee, Bucks Fizz in the morning; beer at the pub. Never mind the sickly dehydration of Monday morning, the anguished recall of a heated debate, the empty wallet, the missing credit card. It all sorted itself out eventually. Besides, there had to be a price for all that fun.

I don't think I ever said no to an invitation to drink – not unless there was a clash of diaries or I had reason to avoid the person doing the inviting.

Alcohol was the main reason for doing anything social. I could liken alcohol to a best friend, but even best friends can lose their appeal if you see too much of them. No matter how often it was around, I never tired of it. Its occasional unexpected absence was a catastrophe for me and I would immediately try to find a bar, or just get away as soon as possible.

I could guzzle a bottle of wine in minutes if left to my own devices. This meant that in slow-drinking company, my frustration could be intense. As soon as I felt the buzz, I wanted another drink and I would keep buying them for everybody in order to keep the flow going.

Alcohol has been the fuel of celebration and consolation all my life. It's given laughter, courage, and opportunity. And because of its power as a fun multiplier, I was willing to entertain all sorts of social invitations: open-mic nights at the pub, seeing bands I'd never heard of, a friend's performance in an am-dram production the other side of London, a goodbye drink at work for someone I'd never even worked with, an invitation to a private reception at a gallery.

You'll never find a better fit than booze and football. I went to hundreds of football matches and watched countless games on the big screens of numerous pubs. I was passionate about football.

Booze was a super-drug. It made a great fist of a disappointing night ahead, and it made a brilliant night legendary.

When It All Started

I don't think my drinking had deeply psychological causes. But maybe I'm not the person to judge such matters. When I think of my childhood, I see it as normal and happy. My parents drank moderately and certainly not every day. I never witnessed drunkenness around me as a boy. On holiday, my parents would have a drink in the hotel bar and then share a bottle of wine at dinner. From the age of about nine, my older sister and I were allowed a glass of wine on the last night of the holiday. This was very exciting.

I was aware of the importance and attraction of alcohol from an early age, and of not being allowed to have any of it. Like most children, I wanted what I couldn't have. Alcohol and cigarettes quickly topped my wish list.

I remember sneaking into my Nan's kitchen to take the best glass from her cupboard and pretending to drink brandy or whisky from it, Grandpa's cigarettes in the other hand. I must have been eight years old at the time.

Alcohol and smoking were the two most grown up activities in the world – and I desperately wanted to do both of them.

I like to think I was a normal kid, able to get on with others and enjoy children's games, but I loved the adult world too and was fascinated by its rituals.

All adult entertainments seemed to involve alcohol, and I wanted to be part of the adult world and all that that entailed. Alcohol was the common denominator.

But it was my first experiences of alcohol outside of the safe family environment that confirmed what the fuss was all about.

I was in a biology class; it was towards the end of the summer term and probably the last biology lesson before summer holidays. Our teacher wanted us to observe, smell, and taste some liquid that we had first experimented with at the beginning of the term, a lesson long forgotten. Apparently we were observing the culmination of the process of fermentation by making beer in school.

The teacher gave us plastic cups so that we could examine the liquid. My eyes shot around the group of white-coated boys for their reaction to the spectacular turn of events. Ambivalence reigned. One boy eyed the contents of the cup with suspicion, tilting it one way, then the other. Another pursed his lips to risk a half mouthful. A third boy spat the contents back into the plastic cup and pulled a face of comic disgust. For fuck's sake, who cared about the taste? This was alcohol, and it was offered to us 14-year-olds in the middle of the day in a classroom by a teacher of all things! I made no secret at my joy of the opportunity to ingest as much home-brew as was my share. I downed a cup and looked around for other thirsty drinkers. It appeared I was something of a spectacle.

There was no guarantee, of course, that this liquid was in any way intoxicating, but I hoped and prayed that it was. We had been given this drink in a classroom, by the teacher, so we had the perfect excuse if things got messy. I remember the excitement of that realisation.

I also remember there was something else going on at this time having to do with my social standing amongst my classmates. I was no longer one of the squares.

So, on that day in biology, when I drank several cups of the foul liquid, one after the other, the unforeseen consequence was the sudden attention on me from all the right people – the ones I most needed to influence. It was an intoxicating feeling! Inhibition was gone, and in its place was a more extroverted version of myself, one I didn't recognise but rather liked.

Then, a few months after the beer incident, still age 14, I was at a friend's house with another mate. It was a Friday afternoon after school. In the garage where we were sitting around chatting, I spotted an unopened bottle of white wine lying on the concrete floor. At my parents' house, all booze was accounted for. Spirits were kept in the living room cabinet, and wine, which had no permanent home of its own and was not in regular supply anyway (not in those days), was kept on the kitchen surface, ready to be consumed the same day it was purchased. So, when I noticed this stray bottle on the garage floor of my friend's house, my heart nearly missed a beat, and I instantly sniffed an opportunity. I asked if the wine was "missing," and my friend, looking a little surprised by my question, seemed to think not. I asked if it would be okay if we drank the wine and he said yes. The thrill was intense.

One of the two lads, I forget which one, picked the bottle up, and with a house key started forcing the cork downwards. It descended about half an inch. I had never seen this done before and never imagined a cork could be forced the wrong way. I was almost bursting with admiration and gratitude. But there was a half-heartedness that crept into his approach when the cork refused to budge any further and I could sense that at any moment the challenge could be abandoned. Everything hung in the balance at that moment, and then, suddenly, the cork plunged into the liquid.

I was the only one of the three of us who wanted the wine, which I drank in large gulps, afraid, irrationally, that my prize would be taken away from me for some reason. I was surprised at how quickly the bottle drained, but I left enough in the bottom so that I could say I hadn't drunk it all. I remember the buzz and the feeling of freedom to say whatever came into my head without worrying about the consequences. I remember the feeling of invincibility on the tube home that evening – a journey I had taken hundreds of times sober, now suddenly transformed into this gregarious, social being, utterly fearless of strangers and at complete ease with himself. Alcohol was a wonderful thing. No wonder every adult drank it so much of the time.

A few months later, I watched the Cup final on the telly at home while my parents were out.

During the game, I took a can of Skol lager from the fridge. It was one of two sitting there waiting to be enjoyed by my mum. I knew the can wasn't mine to take and that its absence would be noticed the moment the fridge door was opened… with consequences. But I must have wanted the lager enough to overlook this fact. I had sipped some beer with my parents in the past, but never had it been family practice for us children to take canned drinks of any kind from the fridge in the middle of the day without parental approval and certainly not beer. The whole thing was unthinkable. But I did it nonetheless. Both cans. With each one I went through the same soul-searching torment before drinking it. I knew I shouldn't have done it, but I couldn't help myself. The opportunity was too great.

Of course the consequences were bad when my mother looked for the beer and found it missing. She must have been so disappointed, which would account for her anger and my shame. It made me feel like a 14-year-old freak, and I hated the disapproval. I would have to be much more careful in the future, I told myself.

From 15 years old onward, I would go to the pub as often as I could get away with it, always with my best friend Bob. He would tell his mum we were going out for a Coke, and she believed him.

We didn't always get away with buying alcohol, but two halves of lager must have been seen by publicans as harmless enough, and besides my mate looked older than his age. We generally had as many halves as we could squeeze in the time. After a while, I told my mum what Bob and I were up to, and she was fine with it. It became the norm. Besides, I wasn't coming home drunk, or late, and I did my school work.

In those early drinking days, I took a lot of positives from alcohol. I wanted to be confident without being cocky. I wanted to talk freely, and beer definitely helped in that department too. Alcohol helped to free the mind without inhibition. Its effects were empowering. I didn't want to worry about life, and alcohol was great at helping me switch off. Socially, it seemed to open doors and everyone wanted to have fun when alcohol was around. No one more than me.

On weekends, Bob and I might meet up with other friends where more alcohol would be available. A bottle of gin might be consumed between a group of seven or eight of us, and if we were lucky there might be a party. What I remember, almost like an imprint in my mind, were the kitchens of every party I ever went to in my teens. I remember the bottles, the plastic cups, the punch bowl, the cans of beer, and the giant tin of Watney's Party 7 pale ale, which no one opened until everything else had run out. I remember because I was always there when it was opened.

I drank so that I could chat to the girls freely without inhibition. I wanted the alcohol to free me. I wanted to be funny and attractive. It was typical teenage stuff, and I don't think I was any different from my peers, but I remember thinking that the alcoholic drinks were a good way to anaesthetise the excruciating awkwardness of trying to talk to people I didn't know.

Of course, it never really worked. Like anyone who tries to shirk the responsibility of being themselves, I was found wanting and failing. You have to put the effort in, learn from your mistakes, and remember what works, so that next time you intuitively know what to do.

But I wasn't interested in learning. I was after a good time. As soon as alcohol made things feel a bit easier, I wanted more of it to ensure I was going to really enjoy the experience. In reality though, it just made conversations more difficult, not less, as I struggled to keep up with what was being said, asking the same basic questions like, "Where are you studying?" in the same loop.

What I failed to grasp was that the feelings of awkwardness in all social settings get easier to deal with the more you practice. I never gave it a chance because I relied on alcohol to take the awkwardness away. For the first few drinks, the strategy worked in the way that it works for everyone, but I never stopped at a few drinks. After several more, my judgement was shot, and my ability to learn or develop social skills was severely impaired. I learned nothing about the kind of girl I wanted to be with or the kinds of conversation that are good in party situations, about humour and empathy or any of the things that ignite friendships.

I never connected alcohol with failure, only with courage and relaxation. Even if my efforts to get a girlfriend always ended in failure, the alcohol made it feel like less of a blow. It became the norm to go out and drink. That's what social activity entailed, and I always had a bit too much of it.

In the second, final year of 6th form college, I actually started seeing a girl. She was dark haired and attractive, quite formal in her manner and dress-sense, but she had warmth. We met in the spacious social area of the college where students hang out drinking coffee and chatting in between classes. Our conversation was polite and unchallenging, largely on account of her first language being not English. She hung around with a group of international students, some Brits too, and on Thursday evenings, we all went off to Trafalgar Square, to the nearby touristy Clarendon Pub in Whitehall. I wasn't sure how attracted I was to Gabrielle, or her to me, and with each visit to this odd choice of venue, the opportunity for our first kiss came and went. We would sing along to the chorus of American Pie and Leaving on a Jet Plane sung by a solo singer dressed as a court jester who roamed the floor of the pub leering at customers as they supped their British ale. The international students loved it and sang along heartily. I loved it too because Gabby let her hair down and sang, and drank beer, and I felt connected with her. But it was fleeting.

The next day we drunk machine-coffee in college and I tried hard to build on the rapport that Gabby and I were letting slip away. I felt incapable of reigniting the spark without all the props to help – the beer, of course, and the jester, the pub, the lions in Trafalgar Square that everyone tried to climb on to when half drunk. Without any of them, Gabrielle and I seemed to have very little in common.

Then I felt it was time to move things on a bit, as she seemed to be getting a little bored, even irritated by my company, which was very disheartening. We had been friendly for three or four weeks but hadn't got any further than idle chit-chat in the lounge area of college, apart from those infrequent Thursday night sing-alongs. So, the next day, I decided to ask her out for a meal, just her and I. I searched for her at the college and spotted her from the top of a crowded stairwell making her way down to the floor below. At first I thought I must have made a mistake, but then I realised what I was seeing was real; she hadn't seen me at this point, so she had no need to conceal her hand holding with another boy, one of the Brits from the Thursday night group at the Clarendon Pub in Whitehall. John was his name. I actually knew him and had considered him a friend. She looked up and saw me and dropped his hand, but we both knew what was happening. I felt sick inside, and my legs suddenly went weak. I caught up with Gabby. I had to. I had already called out to her before realising that she was holding John's hand. I pretended that nothing was wrong, said hello to both of them, babbled something incoherently, and made up an excuse to leave them. And that was it.

I felt like such a failure. I felt angry too. I was angry with myself and also humiliated. It would have felt better if John had been one of the international students. I could have told myself they had more in common with each other. But John was a Brit, and I had thought of myself as superior to him in several ways. I hadn't seen him as a threat. Yet here he was holding Gabby's hand and whatever else he had been up to with her. They looked so comfortable together.

I hated myself. I buried all these feelings deep inside, determined to show that my pride wasn't wounded or even scratched. My other drinking friends, all single boys, were always available for company, and I went off to the reassuring pub to drink beer with them, and everything improved very quickly. I was relieved not to have to worry about Gabrielle anymore or the Clarendon pub full of overseas visitors. It was a ridiculous business anyway. Acting like bloody tourists. So, I forgot all about it. Beer had come to the rescue. That warm glow was always available, and it felt great to be in the bosom of these unchallenging, friendly mates, where conversation flowed and nobody worried about anything. Life was great again very quickly. Besides, there would be plenty of parties ahead. Loads more opportunities.

In the end, I didn't find a girlfriend at 6th form college. I was, however, madly in love with Karen, an 18-year-old classmate in my A-level Sociology class. I spoke to her about eight times over the course of two years, and, once, during class time, I ended up at her bedsit in West London. Yes, she had her own place very close to the college, and four of us went there to smoke weed one afternoon.

I was overflowing with excitement at being in Karen's bedroom with a joint going around the room, but it also felt horrible to think about her sleeping in this room, where her boyfriend could do everything he liked with beautiful Karen. It was horrifying. I had nothing to offer her to lure her away from this bohemian West London world. I was a middle-class boy living at home like everyone else of my age with embarrassing middle-class parents, two sisters, and two dogs. Bedsits were a world away from my deeply unsexy existence. She was living like a rock star compared to me.

I was a virgin too, which only made everything seem

much worse. So, while she was rolling joints and having sex with her boyfriend (he was Mexican and wore a leather choker and smelt of patchouli oil), I was no doubt taking the family dachshunds for a walk or eating macaroni cheese with my parents, watching Starsky & Hutch on TV.

I was too shy to talk to Karen. I think she knew I liked her as I'm sure I turned deep red on all seven of the other occasions we spoke fleetingly between Sociology classes. But I never had the opportunity to socialise with Karen outside of college, so there was never any alcohol around to make me feel more confident. And without alcohol, I wasn't able to really speak to her. I'd love to know what happened to Karen.

What I did get from college, apart from A-levels, was a good knowledge of beer, an ability to chain-smoke, which was very handy in awkward social situations, and a willingness to throw myself into any sort of gathering as long as there was alcohol. I was also happy to sit in pubs all night and talk with mates on any subject. This was all great training for University, which was where I was destined, and where I was desperate to get away to.

University

For many young adults, University is where they discover alcohol. I, on the other hand, had been drinking for several years before I arrived. I felt as though I had an edge over some of my peers, an edge that felt most welcome in the absence of a strong identity of my own. I could fall back on alcohol as a surrogate identity. This was because in addition to all of the confidence-boosting properties of alcohol, my experienced handling of it gave me a certain sophistication which would aid survival on an all-male corridor of 18-year-olds.

At my former inner-London 6th form college, I had studied amidst an eclectic group of international students and West Londoners like myself, of all different ages and backgrounds, and I had felt little or no pressure to conform to a stereotype of any kind. There were no stereotypes. The college felt like a microcosm of London itself.

At this Lancashire University, everything felt very different. I found myself living in a hall of residence on a corridor of young, white males, all of whom seemed to have something to prove to each other. I had no idea what that was, but it was definitely macho, and I knew I wasn't interested in competing.

Alcohol was my saviour in this environment. Not only did it soften the edges, it also gave me a ready-made persona: the southerner who drank heavily without keeling over or throwing up. But when alcohol wasn't around, I felt exposed, tongue-tied by my posh Southern accent.

I was socially relaxed only when half drunk. I lacked

all confidence in the daytime when beer wasn't being consumed. Fortunately, alcohol was always available at social gatherings. This was its purpose and why everyone drank it. Everyone needed a bit of 'Dutch courage.' But I really missed it when it wasn't available.

As a result of this, I drank every day at University, without fail. On one occasion I went with a group of new friends on a coach trip organised by one of the many University clubs – it was a picnic in the country where everyone was given a sandwich, a bag of crisps, and a bottle of wine each. I was impressed with the organiser's thinking, but a bit worried that one bottle of wine wouldn't be quite enough, and we might be stuck in the middle of nowhere without any back-up supplies. There was nothing I could do about it, so off we went on the coach.

To my complete horror, when we arrived at our destination, everyone on this coach party saved their wine, ate their picnic in complete sobriety, sat around chatting for what seemed like an eternity, and then got back on the coach to go home. It was a terrible shock, and I couldn't believe that anyone would want to sit around chatting while looking at, but not drinking, their own wine.

I agonised whether to open my own bottle, but somehow couldn't muster enough courage to do so. I could think of nothing else. I just couldn't believe these people had actually come on a picnic to sit around chatting over a sandwich.

During my time at university I squandered the many chances that a busy social life offered me to get in touch with my 'inner self' – to find out what occasions I liked best, and which sorts of people and activities. So dependent was I on alcohol to make me feel more confident, I found myself socialising only with heavy drinkers. Alcohol was always there to anaesthetise any pain. I was lazy and took the easy option.

Pour alcohol into me and I could enjoy hours spent sitting around in bars and clubs. Heavy drinking became part of my identity, I guess, and saved me from trying to find a real one. So, I never learned the social nuances of what worked and what didn't in a social encounter, when to walk away and when to jump in. My reactions were fuelled by alcohol, so when it was absent, I didn't feel confident in how to react or behave. I felt awkward.

I had one relationship with a girl in the whole three years I was at University. Kathleen. It lasted a full academic year, which I see as something of an achievement. There was clearly a mutual attraction, but the dynamics were all wrong from the start. Such was my low self-esteem, I was surprised and grateful that she liked me, so I was too keen to please her and fit in with her wishes. I was so unsure of what I wanted in a relationship that I ended up trying to give Kathleen what she wanted.

She came into the relationship with more self-esteem than me. She had left a boyfriend back in her hometown before coming to University, and I became increasingly unsure as time went on that this boy was ever truly out of the picture. Where sex was concerned, Kathleen was all buttoned up. Our encounters never amounted to much more than a bit of fumbling around. Eventually, she told me it was all due to the highly physical relationship she still had back home. It was a blow to the gut receiving this information. I refused to give away any feelings of hurt in all of this, however, so I just acted as though it made little difference to me. I didn't know how to convey my feelings without getting angry or without feeling vulnerable.

In addition to this, she had a number of male admirers who would invite her out, and from time to time she would accept their invitations coquettishly, leaving me seething and squirming with jealousy but unable to confront her about it in an adult way. I have no doubt she was trying to tease a reaction out of me. It failed.

Then, one time after drinking heavily with my mates I wrote her an angry letter, a very formal one at that, outlining how despicable she had been. The letter was perfectly crafted and designed to leave her feeling terrible about herself.
To my great relief, she knocked on my door the next day having read my outpourings and, with a naughty-girl-look on her face, asked for forgiveness.

It was exactly what I had hoped for, and after an agonisingly long wait for her to come around to my room, we instantly made up. Since I was so grateful for this and didn't wish to rock the boat any further, I brushed away her attempts at discussing my letter. I tried to forget all negativity and instead move forward so that our relationship could continue on its wobbly course.

When things felt good between us, I was sure we would be together forever. When they were bad, it was because I thought she had lost interest in me and was itching to get away. In the summer of our graduation, she came to London to visit me and to tell me it was all over.

I look back now at my time spent at University like it was an assault course. Everything felt so raw at 18, and alcohol was definitely the anaesthetic to all those social wounds. I scraped by with a degree and accrued big debt, which was shameful considering the generous grant system at the time. I felt the bigger achievement was survival. Sure, I had some good times, all of them when drunk, but there was so much wastage of every kind, I can't say I feel proud of any of it. I certainly don't think I was ever truly happy.

People look back to their college days as a time when they were able to come out of their shell and grow. Instead, I turned inward and drank.

Working For A Living

University had one thing going for it at least: the sense of freedom. This came to an abrupt end when I entered the working world of tele-sales. My life had suddenly regressed to primary school again. My whole day seemed to be under varying degrees of scrutiny and time-management, including, it seemed, my bladder and bowel frequency. Once the novelty of a paycheque had been wiped out by London rent, and the draconian rules of a 9-5, Monday-to-Friday existence at the foot of the employment ladder had eaten into my spirit, I began to wonder if the rest of my life was going to be this awful. I started dreaming about getting rich. I wanted my freedom back, but I wanted and needed the salary to go with it.

I figured that my escape route out of mediocrity and debt lay in the music industry. Well, my old University friend's band, more precisely, in which I played the drums. Like many other fledgling groups, we just needed a lucky break. Our hobby gradually became our only hope while the loathsome day-job paid the bills and stole our time. Most nights, instead of pursuing our dream into the early hours, we went to the pub where we would discuss plans for our breakthrough, when it happened.

The few hours per week that were actually spent in a rehearsal studio never progressed much further than the odd demo-tape which was sent off to record companies with very little perseverance or follow-up. Evidently, whether I realised it or not, I wasn't willing to fight for success. We *would* take *no* for an answer and slope off to the pub to lick our wounded egos. Consolation for rejection was waiting at the end of the road... in the pub, where therapy and hope were served in pint pots and all sorts of new plans could be hatched, discussed, and re-worked until closing time.

By 11 p.m. most nights, we started to believe we were within a whisker of making it. Booze was both fuelling the dreams and smoothing the disappointments.

But tension grew when the main man in the band, whom I lived with in a post-student house-share, and I had a falling out. Accusations of non-commitment flew around as jobs and rent were juggled alongside rehearsal time. This escape route from the prison of an office job became a prison itself, and I just had to get out. Alcohol became a salvation, and I went off to the pub each night to pursue it. Alcohol was always a salvation.

I finally escaped my housemate and the band and carried on with the office-bound sales job for several years, motivated only by evening and weekend sessions in the pub.
My ambitions for making easy money never diminished though, and in my late 20s and early 30s, I got involved in the first of a number of make-

money-quick network marketing schemes. These were in addition to the day job and promised only 10 to 16 hours of work a week to get them underway and start raking in the cash. In all, I tried about five schemes over the course of the next 10 years. They all failed.

They started with the oh-so-important task of writing down your goals, your wish list of wild desires designed to spur you on when motivation levels dropped. You were supposed to look at your list of goals, pinned by fridge magnets lest you ever forget them – the yacht, the villa, the fast cars, the designer clothes and jewellery – and you'd be reinvigorated and raring to go again.

I would fantasize about meeting up with my mates in the middle of the day and sitting in a boozer all afternoon. If I forced myself to dream about living abroad, a seedy one-bed Barcelona apartment and a crate of Rioja would be all I needed. My ambitions went no further than being able to afford the time and money for drinking. But the wish list of luxury items didn't really excite me.

In the real world, the network marketing schemes were supposed to be fitted into the remaining hours after the proper day job had ended. But I needed a drink too. I had to have a drink at the end of each day; a bit of me time. We all need that, don't we? Besides, drinking was part and parcel of life, as important as having a roof over my head, food to eat, friends and family to love and be loved by, and a job to pay for it all. It had to fit in, come what may. No scheme, however much it promised, could take away my time for alcohol. Not for too long anyway. Consequently, they all failed.

Money and alcohol were always on my mind. How was I going to fund the months ahead, if I even thought that far into the future?

For colleagues, a salary covered the cost of rent and a social life as well as nice things like new clothes, holidays, hobbies, gym membership, nice presents and a few savings left over. My salary and all sources of financial credit, whether bank overdraft, bank loan or credit card, was swallowed up by alcohol. The job, after all, was a means to an end. I had no interest in what I did for a living as long as I was reasonably good at it and it continued to pay for my life-style. So, my ambitions were low. I always wanted to stay within my comfort zone. I shouldn't have been surprised that I didn't progress throughout my career in sales. I could do each job well enough, but my ability to analyse what I was getting from each one was clouded by alcohol.

Furthermore, the erratic nature of a basic salary plus commission was fine for me as there was always the possibility of a wind-fall bonus to clear debts accrued through my excessive lifestyle. I felt okay with sinking into the red as there was always the prospect that a bumper month would get me straight again.

Media sales jobs suited me because they paid well enough for minimal work done. They rewarded salespeople for success not work, which was largely carried out by other people once the sale was made, and that's when I, legitimately, would be in the pub!

I chopped and changed homes in the decade after I finished University, living with mates for a while, then moving in with a girlfriend for slightly less time, and in between returning to Mum and Dad's place temporarily. I had no life plan or ambition. I lurched from one set of circumstances to the next. I was happy enough, but I lived a day-to-day existence, planning the odd holiday and certainly a few celebratory occasions, but my real concerns were for what I, or we (whoever else was involved at the time), would be doing later that evening. I realised that not everyone would want to gather in a rundown pub every night and go for a curry afterwards, so some planning would be required, and that's what I focussed on. The other stuff just happened. I was always in financial debt and was always surviving on bailouts from my mum, who seemed to know when things were tight. I never had to ask.

Other people my age and in my group of friends gradually got married and started families, and that would have been fine for me too, if it had "happened" to me. But it didn't. And I didn't try to make it happen. I lived day to day. I was more concerned with creating great moments to live in the memory.

For years, I acted much like a Border Collie with a herd of sheep – skilfully rounding up my charges and carefully directing them towards and into the bar, time and time again, as though it were the only important place to go. I almost always made too much of these occasions, getting their significance completely out of proportion.

I should have spent far more time concentrating on my ambitions, my next steps, finding a girlfriend, settling down, getting married, and starting a family. Instead, I kept planning my next great night out.

Middle-Aged, Middle-Class Drinker

Apart from one or two serious, but short, romances, I have been single for much of my adult life. I always had stronger friendships than relationships. Alcohol and friendship goes much better together than alcohol and partnership.

I went on occasional dates and had the odd fling, but nothing much came of such encounters. They were invariably arranged when both parties were drunk, so the match was often based on all the wrong criteria.
But alcohol would give me the courage to talk to women in the first instance, so I always relied on its

support. It was unthinkable not to drink on a date. What would we say to each other?

Long into my 30s, I was introduced to a wonderful girl on a blind date, and the chemistry between us flowed. We had been matched by a close mutual friend. My date knew in advance that I was a drinker, and she herself had a reputation as a party girl. We went into the evening prepared for things to happen between us. Rachel was beautiful.

The sparkling drinks did their magic, and we chatted and flirted our way through a bottle of cava and a large glass of Pinot Grigio. Then, at her favourite cocktail bar, we chatted some more, but I was struggling to keep up with the conversation and went into one of my interrogation loops where I ask the same questions, one after the other, not listening to or remembering the answers.

Two more glasses of champagne later, we decided to hit Soho. Of course, I was drinking on an empty stomach. I had already had a bottle of wine before meeting Rachel. So, in Soho, I bought her a margarita and ordered a sparkling water for myself. But it was too late. I didn't even know where I was. Returning with our drinks, I couldn't find Rachel anywhere in the bar and I was spilling the margarita. When I spotted her at last, she was talking to strangers animatedly. She knew I was wasted. She must have. All I remember is telling her I had to leave.

I woke up on a bench at 3am in a part of London I had never been to before, 12 miles from home. I think I caught a bus at some point. She thought it was funny, so I am led to understand. I didn't see her again in person for quite some time, not until after she was married. The evening had been just a bit of fun, nothing more. But it might have been the start of something. I had blown my chance. The fact was, when it came to pure choice, no strings, I wouldn't choose anything so precious that needed me to stay sober. So I concluded she wasn't for me.

It's a bit of a relief when one day you realise you have grown into, and now comfortably fit the mould of, the single, middle-aged man. Without having to do anything in particular other than carry on as before, I had shrugged the label that read 'overgrown student' for the more pleasing 'pub-loving bachelor'. It's a status I conferred on myself, no doubt, but it fitted like a glove, and nobody challenged it.

I no longer struggled with the idea of having to work a 9-5 existence, and although I had no real ambition career-wise, I quite enjoyed my life in sales. I still embarked on network marketing schemes from time to time, none of which made any money, but despite that, I was reasonably content.

I was able to exert some discipline on my drinking, in that I stayed off alcohol all day, but I drank from the moment I finished work, either with colleagues or on my own at various pubs and bars on the way home. By the time I walked through the front door with some food and a bottle of wine, it was past 8 p.m., and so I would carry on drinking while preparing an evening meal, which I would eat with a bottle of wine watching news programs on TV. On weekends, attending live football matches would ensure an early start in the pub on Saturdays followed by steady drinking at various points during the afternoon, which would lead into the evening's entertainment, whatever that was; it really wasn't important as long I had refreshments.

On Sundays, if I had done my preparations, I would go for lunch with friends somewhere. Alcohol would always be a feature at some point in the day and would be anticipated all the way up to the first drink. Whether I was living alone or with friends, this was the pattern by and large. Having people around made it more sociable, but it didn't alter my drinking consumption significantly.

The increase in solitary drinking meant that I would drink a bit too much before social occasions and then peak too early. I now had a reputation for falling asleep at parties.

Then I started to rely on alcohol even more. Things happened that made it seem okay to drink at times that I would have considered not sensible in the past (I'll elaborate more in the upcoming section on drinking alone and secret drinking). I started to feel that all activity, not just social activity, was better when alcohol was involved. I became less interested in big social occasions where I was guaranteed to get drunk and my mood to swing in favour of ordinary daily life where a drink or two might spice things up, unnoticed by anyone around me.

Perhaps I was on a slippery slope by this stage. I don't know. I still felt pretty much in control.

One thing that wasn't always in control anymore was my mood. From time to time, I would find an outlet for all my bottled-up resentments. And that time was when I had been drinking heavily. My sarcasm would take control, fuelled by a conviction that everyone around me was against me in some way.

Partly because of this dangerous new development with my mood, I decided it was for the best to attempt a dry January. I was by now in my mid 40s. Along with many other heavy drinkers at the start of a new year, following a heavy December, the prospect of a break from alcohol was almost desirable. I stayed in every night and eat as much food as I could manage and watched hours of TV eating ice cream.

With alcoholic temptation removed, I got through the first few days without too much difficulty. I started to plan how I would return to moderate drinking at the end of the month. The strange thing is, I told myself not to get too used to this eerily calm feeling, as I would be needing alcohol again when normal, drinking life resumed. I didn't challenge the need for alcohol just because I was enjoying my time away from it. I knew its overall importance in my life. Just that for now, I thought it best to cleanse the system for a short while. It all seemed rather easy. With my priorities better aligned, I thought this would be a good time to settle down with a girlfriend.

Incredibly luckily, I met and fell in love with the woman who would become my life partner. Jane and I are still together today.

When I went back to moderate drinking at the end of that dry January, now with Jane in my life, the moderation didn't last beyond a few days. And it wasn't too long before alcohol became a problem for me.
Even having cut down, I was still at the upper levels of Jane's drinking range. There was no way I was going to keep things going in the manner I had become accustomed to, so I had to find a way of keeping my drinking under control, yet at the same time at satisfactory levels. This was quite difficult to achieve and made me tense and irritable on many occasions, with near-disastrous consequences.

One night, I was late meeting her at the tube station. We were going to see a band at the Forum in North London. I had already had a couple of drinks, hence why I was running late. Jane was in a bad mood after waiting for me, and I hate being disapproved of. I was angry with myself for getting the timing wrong but angry with Jane because she knew very well how unpredictable rush-hour travel is. She wasn't to know I had been in the pub. So, I was in a foul temper, which I kept tightly bottled up.

We had planned on getting a snack, but by this point, all I wanted was a drink, a proper drink. I'd have been quite happy to say fuck it to the band and sit in the pub all night. Fortunately, every eatery was either rammed or not quite "right," so we settled for a supermarket sandwich. Then we went to the pub and I joined the wall of bodies waiting at the bar. Queuing for a drink when there's time for only one is such a depressing waste.

Once inside the music venue, I remembered there was a bar at the back of the auditorium. I have never felt so relieved. So, I gulped cider frantically and things felt better but got much worse. I made a joke that was met with disdain and the tension between us started gripping my throat. Alienation took hold. How dare she disapprove of me! The loathsome gig droned on. It was new song after new song when all I had wanted and paid for were the famous ones. I was furious on the inside, and it wasn't going to stay there.

Jane turned to me. "Well, that was good," she said, eager to break the silence with anything at all.

"I thought it was fucking shit," I replied.

"Oh, I'm sorry," she said, visibly and audibly shocked, her voice trailing off into a whisper.

Everything was running away from me. I had lost it. I knew that what I was about to do I would regret, but I was powerless to stop the flow of bile coming out of me. My drunken, swollen sense of dignity had been punched, and I couldn't just stand silently by. I had my pride. I knew she would walk out on me, maybe forever, but on I went. All my pent-up anger from various moments of recent indignation came spewing out, the whole taxi ride home and again inside the house where I drank more despite her pleading with me not to. She left me that night, and I didn't know what was happening. I drank more vodka and then passed out.

Somehow, against all the odds, I made up with Jane a few days later. She forgave me, I think. I knew I had let alcohol get control of me, and I vowed to check my behaviour in future. I needed to make sure this didn't happen again. In Jane's eyes, I'm sure she felt it probably would. But I couldn't wipe it from history. I made sure I was well behaved after that. In reality, however, neither of us really knew if and when this kind of outburst might erupt.

Something had changed; my reliable crutch alcohol was no longer so reliable. It did things to my mind and my behaviour which it hadn't done before, or not as extremely, and yet I needed more and more of it.

Drinking Alone

In my 20s, I was loathe to drink alone, at least at the start. The fact is I was very rarely alone, living in a shared accommodation, but by 27 years old, I had bought a small flat (with an exceedingly big loan – this was the 1980s, of course) and was living by myself. I drank by myself quite often too, now that I had my own place, and drinking alone in the flat felt both very grown up and slightly lonely at the same time. Usually, having poured a few drinks, I would wander off to the pub for more drinks. I wouldn't have gone to the pub on my own, sober.

As I got into my 30s, I dropped into pubs on my own regularly. At the start, it didn't feel very comfortable though. I would have a debate in my head whether what I was doing was normal, not alcoholic. But I soon got into the swing. I looked out for pubs to visit, the scruffier the better, and I would seek out a lone drinker at the bar and drink near them so that conversation would spring up. It was always old blokes I spoke with on these occasions, blokes who were grateful for someone to listen to their memories of how things were in the 50s. This was educational for me and enjoyable for both of us. I came away feeling good about myself; it's what people did. I had seen them, and now I told myself it would be alright for me to do it too which was a way of masking the fact I had been drinking alone in the pub during the day.

As with all my drinking, drinking alone was about getting to a certain level of intoxication and then stopping. That was always the plan. I never wanted to drink to blackout or to pass out. I just wanted enough to feel great, and then I would be satisfied. I would usually start out with a strong sense of how much alcohol I would need to get me to the desired 'high' – half a bottle of spirit or a bottle of wine. Once that was consumed, I would feel great and would be ready to eat. Except that having drunk the wine or the spirit, I would want more of it because the 'high' rarely materialised when I expected it to or I wouldn't recognise it when it was upon me. So, I always needed a bit more. I would go out and buy another bottle of wine or a half bottle of spirit rather than eat my dinner and curb my thirst for alcohol.

Food was a guaranteed foot-brake on my drinking, one that I could apply whenever I felt ready to. Knowing that it was there gave me a sense of control. Rarely, if ever, did I actually use it. Sometimes, I would go out twice in the evening to buy more alcohol. The second time, all judgement and control would have disappeared and I would buy a full bottle of spirit and another two bottles of wine. The next day, I would awaken and see all this leftover alcohol and think about how self-controlled I must have been. That's until I looked at my bank balance and credit card receipts.

I used to really enjoy drinking alone at home in my late thirties. I could invent all sorts of games and fantasies to amuse myself.

For example, on holiday, getting ready to go out in the evening whilst sipping a gin and tonic in the bathroom, I'd imagine that I was a famous film star and the villa I was staying in, my private apartment… it's all part of the drinking fun, isn't it?

If ever I had a Friday evening to myself, I would look forward to a night at home with plenty of red wine, some vodka, and a bag full of supermarket shopping. The plan would be to have a good drink followed by a delicious roast dinner. I could listen to my favourite radio station while I drank and cooked.

I would pour the first vodka, a very stiff measure, indulging myself in a fantasy world in order to spice the evening up. I would pretend I was, say, a 1930s Secretary of State.

After polishing off the first vodka, I would have a sudden urge to giggle. It was my brain loosening its grip on my limbs as the vodka arrived. Things could only get better.
I would sit at the kitchen table trying to catch up with my thoughts, which would, by this stage, start to run away from the planned fantasy. I'd open the wine and get the chicken in the oven, put some music on, and drink the wine quickly.

I would cook and drink and maybe make some phone calls to friends, planning the weekend ahead. I would drink some more and slow down the cooking process as I wouldn't want the impending food to quash the evening's fun. Then I'd plate my food and leave it in the oven for when I was finally ready to eat. I'd maybe have another small vodka before going back to the wine.

The rest would be a blur. My Secretary of State fantasy long forgotten, I would fall asleep on the sofa fully clad, plates of half-finished food all around me. The evening and the meal would be wasted, and mounds of washing and cleaning up would await me in the morning. But I would have kept out of bars and pubs and restaurants that night – my consolation for spoiling the start of the weekend.

The following morning, I might go for a run before cleaning up the mess from the night before and would then reward myself with a trip to the pub where all my football supporter pub-friends would be starting to gather. These friends made me feel much better about myself where alcohol was concerned. They always seemed to drink more than me, which was very reassuring.

I thought nothing of drinking alone. Over the years, pubs have got more and more expensive and supermarkets cheaper and cheaper. Besides, I loved the idea of pouring a gin and tonic when I got home from work. But of course, it was never just one. The pleasure of the first gin always fell slightly short, so I would keep trying to chase the buzz through the evening.

If only I had learned how to enjoy the first drink of the night, things might have been different. Once I had started seeking that buzz, I couldn't just give up.

On a weeknight, I would at least recognise that I couldn't keep chasing the buzz all evening, so I would try to adopt my rescue strategy – eating a proper meal – a bit earlier than I would have liked, but it was a battle I had with myself nightly, the battle of when to admit that the buzz wasn't worth chasing anymore. Sometimes, very often in fact, I would wake up the next morning with no memory of having eaten anything the night before, not until I saw the food wrappers in the bin. It was a mixed blessing. Yes, I had eaten, but so late in the end that I had forgotten doing it.

The medical profession makes such a fuss about drinking on your own, but many people don't have the money or the social circle to drink in bars. Where else are they to drink other than in the safety of their own home? I knew that most of my friends drank on their own, so I didn't think of myself as unusual. I did occasionally check the literature on safe limits but concluded that they were so low as to be meaningless.
Everybody drank more than that. The people who

drank within the safe limits were practically teetotal and certainly never worried about their drinking. Much of the literature on alcoholism or dependency talked about physical need for alcohol, to steady a shaking hand, including in the mornings. I never had this need, so I felt I was alright.

Secret Drinking

I started drinking on daily commutes after a long journey from Manchester had been spiced up in the buffet car and I realised that drinking on the underground was no different in principle than drinking on National Rail.

On the underground, the drinking had to be kept secretive because it was illegal, but it wasn't any trouble disguising alcoholic drinks.

As I got into my 40s, I would take more and more disguised hooch with me on journeys. It cheered the travel inconvenience immensely, and it became almost a daily routine for me on return journeys from work.

I think I was able to appreciate the buzz more distinctly when I was trying to be completely sober. This was true not only of journeys, but once I had reached my destination too.

It was quite an inconvenience to me if I had to travel anywhere with a friend because it meant I couldn't drink – unless it was late at night, in which case I would make jest that the "travel bar" was open and would offer a range of alcoholic beverages to my friends to their great merriment.

I loved the idea that people would imagine me as a human drinks trolley. It was part of the heavy-drinking persona that I encouraged, hinting at alcoholic behaviour but in an amusing way – much like the vodka I bought for our shared house, a supermarket own-brand with a label that just said "Vodka" and nothing else. It was all part of the hilarious "irony" that told everyone I drank too much but didn't care. It conveyed how comfortable I was with celebrating the loss of my own dignity.

Whenever I looked up at the booze corner at home, on top of the dresser, there would always be less than I remembered. The vodka bottle that should have been almost full was, in fact, almost empty. I feared always that my housemates would know that I had nipped away at this supply in the daytime. I very much cared about that and was certainly not celebrating the loss of my own dignity by letting them find out. I didn't want anyone to know I was ashamed or appeared to be out of control.

I would pour the vodka into a glass making sure I could see how much the bottle had been reduced so that I could top it back off to the same level later on and cover my tracks. If I had run out of cheap tonic or Coke, I might make do with iced water. Or just plain water on some occasions.

Being in control of how others viewed my drinking was very important to me. Although how I thought I was achieving it was surely self-delusional.

By my mid-40s, I would have a secret drink whenever and wherever I gave myself the green light. The general rule was this: I wouldn't drink on the way to work in the mornings – unless I had high anxiety and had given myself permission to do so – permission being based on whether I had a clear day ahead of me, so that I could get through it on autopilot.

If I was suffering high anxiety in the morning, such as after a shameful drunken rant the night before, I would fix myself a small drink or two to help me feel better able to deal with the aftermath. Without alcohol, you tend to think things through too much. You analyse all of the consequences. After a couple of drinks, you are able to shut some of that out and concentrate on the task at hand.

I could send a few apologetic texts and gauge how badly I had caused offense. A drink would loosen the tongue and generate some emotion, making a heart-felt apology easier. [It was no less heart-felt, just better and more easily delivered.]

Early morning vodka always gave me an urge to giggle – like a hiccup. It was the booze fiddling with my factory settings. It was the only time I could guarantee a real high, but I would continue to chase it all day, hoping for a second buzz, always in vain.

Once I had given myself the go-ahead to drink, I couldn't do anything else until the desire was satisfied. I quite liked the shed at the bottom of my garden. I could smoke and drink inside it, and nobody need know I was there. I had started to hide booze in the shed as well as many of my empty bottles and cans.

The shed was a vital outpost in my operations from home. It was also the hub of my secret drinking. In the winter, nobody ever went in there except for me. I loved it.

But my shed could only be used during phases in my life when I was based at home. At other times, I was working 9-5 at my employers' offices, usually in Central London. I missed the freedom of working from home, when I was so employed.
I figured a good compromise was to allocate the odd day, here and there, to secret drinking at work but only under my own strict rules. I was determined to be in total control, making sure that everything went smoothly, and that nobody found out what I was doing. I found that it was possible to spice up the day by drinking secretly while pretending to be sober. I'm not really a risk taker in life, so this wasn't about the excitement of gambling.

I was absolutely not prepared to be found out and certainly not willing to be confronted – that was unthinkable. I needed to be certain that I could get away with it. Lots of chewing gum helped see to that. On the way to work, I would buy miniature bottles of vodka from newsagents and pour one or two of them at a time into a 500ml plastic bottle of strawberry Volvic water which I drank at my work station. I even took the bottle into meetings.

Some days, I started drinking before I arrived at work. Other days, I would purchase the kit at lunchtime after a few drinks in the pub.

The thing is, I didn't need to do it, and if I had been required to do anything remotely out of my comfort zone at work, then I wouldn't have been so stupid as to have played this game – which is all it was in my mind.

It was a game that alleviated the dullest of dull days. Even before arriving at work, those first swigs of hooch had a special effect because of the heightened awareness at eight in the morning. I really noticed the buzz I was getting from the drink, far more so than in the evening when alcoholic fuzziness was more the norm than a state of sobriety. Everyone and everything looked a bit more interesting, like looking at your surroundings whilst listening to music through earphones.

I felt a little thrill at the prospect of saying hello to

colleagues on arrival, and with good reason. As soon as I walked through the building to my workstation, all that clunkiness evaporated. I felt free from social awkwardness, and the beauty was that even if someone thought you were acting a little differently, they would never suspect booze because no one drinks at eight in the morning at work.

My challenge was to behave in a sober manner. Meetings were transformed. No matter how dull they were, they could be spiced up by secret hooch. Occasionally, I could feel the effects of the vodka too keenly and would stop drinking for a while, have a coffee and drink some normal water, after which the secret drinking could resume.

Secretive drinking was a way of spicing up work and travel, but it also had the very practical function of intoxicating myself to a sufficient level that only a modest top up was needed to reach the overall required quantity for the evening. So, I would drink secretively before arriving home or at a social gathering, just so that I needn't worry about the booze running out or looking like I was drinking more than anyone else. I would have already drunk sufficient quantity to get me to a comfortable level. But getting that level right was sometimes hard. I often miscalculated.

At home, I had bottles of booze in various hideaways, and I would disappear from time to time in the evening to have a nip or a glug at them. Almost always spirits and sometimes wine, and always in small bottles for easy stow-away and disposal.

Never, not once, did a secret supply of alcohol get discovered at home. I did get caught on the train a few times, however, by colleagues who came to sit with me as I abandoned open drinks on the floor, pretending they weren't mine. A client once saw me on the First Capital train out of Moorgate station with a can of cider in my hand, which was embarrassing as we both pretended we hadn't seen each other, a charade that lasted six stops before I got off, looking theatrically absorbed in all things that weren't within two feet of where he was standing.

Secret drinking never seemed all that wrong to me. I think because I rationalised it so much, setting rules around when I'd allow it and when I wouldn't, I felt I had complete control over what I was doing. Control was key. Alcoholics don't have control of their drinking. So as far as I was concerned, I didn't have a problem.

The Bits I Tried to Forget

When I started to write *Not Alcoholic, But...* I considered myself to be as the title hints: not alcoholic, but... a (reformed) heavy drinker. So, I began the process of writing down all my experiences around alcohol up to the point when I stopped drinking. I was trying to make sense of what I had done and what had motivated me to such action. It was a therapeutic endeavour out of which I hoped to be able to share some insights for the benefit of other heavy drinkers.

It wasn't until later on that I realised I had left out a large and destructive chunk of my drinking, one that I had buried, one that revolved around my mother and her drinking over a period of about 25 years. I tried to brush it under the carpet all of my adult life. Here in this book about my drinking history, I feel the need to share it, largely because I'm sure it says much about the nature of my drinking problem.

During my childhood, my mother wasn't a heavy drinker. Alcohol was a treat for both my parents and they drank it on special occasions only. As a family, we were sociable and popular, in touch with wider family members, we went on holiday each year to meet up with the same people, and had lots of friends who we saw regularly.

My mum was a great confidant, highly intuitive and capable of uplifting-empathy. But she was also super sensitive. She could detect the slightest change in someone's greeting, or the level of enthusiasm in their voice. She and I would analyse these almost imperceptible changes of attitude in a family friend's body language or tone for hours at a stretch, during which time I learnt a lot about my mother's lack of confidence beneath her loud and quite boisterous surface.

As a teenager I found it empowering to be such a significant person in my mother's life, sharing with her the nuances of friends and family interaction, but I wasn't aware that I was occupying a role that my mother should have relied on her own peers to fulfil. She wasn't sharing her thoughts and fears with anyone else but me, and I don't think it was healthy for her.

I didn't realise at the time how damaging it was that she had no one else in her life to prop her up. When I look back at her diaries now, I see she had quite a sociable time over the years that I and my sisters were growing up. But I don't remember my mother talking about her feelings to anyone. If she had problems, none of her friends knew about them. She bottled them all up.

As she neared middle age her sensitivity got worse, not better, and her confidence shrank. She started to believe that all her family and friends were disapproving of her whilst sympathising with my father. On the surface she just about managed to keep it all together, but I could feel the growing tension. Around this time, I noticed too that my mother's mood changed with alcohol. After one drink she would relax, enough to open up a little, say something amusing, perhaps a bit controversial. But after two, her mood turned negative and she might pick out and repeat something I had said earlier in the day, or even weeks ago, and contrive some hidden agenda on my part, the alcohol goading her to vocalise her innermost fears. If I protested, her argument would get entrenched and then a battle would be on the cards. Things spiralled out of control quickly in these circumstances. Alcohol was the fuse, the spark, the explosive and the fire.

The big change for the worse happened when my grand-father, her father, died. It was like the lancing of a great boil. Some of her relatives felt the need to get things off their chest. Old grievances came out and things were said. Accusations of bullying and dishonesty were levelled at my mother and she decided that the world believed them unequivocally. She also decided that my father had sided with the enemy. Now this had a very significant effect on everything that followed. It meant that from now on, anyone who showed friendliness towards my father was ipso facto against her. It was a contorted logic that found its voice after several glasses of white wine.

Alcohol offered my mother the courage to vocalise her fears where previously, when sober, she had bottled them up. Alcohol released her from her own shackles and at once she became eager to test her newly found confidence. Fearless. She would drink heavily and phone family and friends to tell them what she had been called by her enemies. When they responded coolly to her belligerent tone, she would take this as a sure sign they too were against her. She would practically goad them into saying defensive things about my father.

When they did so, her tone would harden further. Very often the people she phoned had no idea how they were expected to react. It was a recipe for disaster. It was the surest self-fulfilling prophecy that ever existed, and she couldn't see it. She couldn't bear to admit that alcohol had got a hold of her. She could only see that she was upset and that the wine "might not have helped." She had reason to be upset – her family had said and done some terrible things, but her drunken responses – always angry – were destroying her credibility. Somehow, she didn't seem to think it mattered, her drunkenness, that it shouldn't detract from her case against her treacherous sister and brother-in-law. Besides, she needed the alcohol to give her the courage to speak out, even though it all seemed to go wrong when she did. The whole thing spiralled out of control, and she never got to grips with it.

She would claim that her enemies had "got away with it." She never saw that her repeated door stepping of them and drunk phone calls encouraged such an outcome. She felt that her drinking "paled into insignificance" (another of her favourite phrases) in comparison to her sister and brother-in-law's libellous accusations of dishonesty towards her, so she didn't feel the need to temper her response. However, these libellous comments always got overlooked by the outside world while the finger of blame pointed at her drunken behaviour, and she was again outraged.

Drinking was also her consolation. She drank heavily after these episodes to make her feel better about herself, to make it bearable, and then the rage would take hold once more and round she'd go again in another cycle. Round and round it went.

In time, she realised she had lost all her relationships and friends but would phone them anyway, buoyed up after a few drinks. Her tone would be defensive from the outset. The negative response she received was proof to her that they were against her. It was almost a relief for her now. It's what she knew already. They put the phone down on her or made an excuse and got off the line. She would tell me afterwards what had happened in a sort of cock-sure I-told-you-so manner. I think she knew her drunkenness contributed to the negative reception, but she felt the battle was lost anyway so it didn't matter.

I knew how badly she had been treated, but I could see how catastrophically she was dealing with it and tried to tell her. She couldn't understand why I wasn't as outraged as she was by the treachery heaped upon our family, and she took my constructive criticism of her drunken phone calls to everybody, including me, as a sign of my defection to the other side. She was wrong to believe I had defected from her, and we would fight over it bitterly, fuelled by wine.

Alcohol made us see everything in black and white.

No shades.

Our spats would never start when sober. We would be in unison to begin with. We would discuss the awfulness of the family situation (it was always awful in my mother's eyes) in complete agreement with one another, analysing each and every nuanced comment, all the hidden subtext, each lie, blasphemy, and slander by our traitorous wider family. Then the wine would come out. The wine played its tricks. It put doubts into my mother's head about even my own loyalty to her, and she would start to turn on me, snarling, "You think it's all just in the past and doesn't matter," or "You think exactly the same as your father, that I've got the whole thing out of proportion." She always "knew" my motives once the wine kicked in. We would be heading for a row now.

My mother was adamant that she knew exactly what other people's opinion of her was. Because of her low self-esteem, she believed whole-heartedly that all opinions of her, including mine, were negative. I would have to put up a great performance to convince her to the contrary, but it was impossible. She would already have made up her mind that I thought she was in the wrong, and she would twist my words to prove her point. It drove me wild with anger, which the wine only fuelled.

Where was my father in all this? He was physically present but bewildered. Not being blessed with much empathy, his responses showed how mystified he was by what was going on around him. He once confided in me, in all sincerity, that he had seen a correlation between the lunar chart and my mother's outbursts. He was deadly serious.

His contribution to family arguments and his responses to them were prone to misinterpretation – something my mother specialised in anyway. He was prone to say the same provocative remarks over and over again without understanding how this would inflame my mother's anger, not temper it. I couldn't understand my father's motives. Was he deliberately winding her up so as to give himself the opportunity to storm out of the flat, something he did often when the heat got too much for him, or was he deliberately goading her out of sheer malice?

Long before I realised how emotionally rudderless he was, I drunkenly decided he was evil not stupid and tried to hit him in the middle of a family meltdown. It was the only row that turned physically violent although I was so drunk I failed to connect the single punch I attempted to inflict on him. He took himself off to bed in response. The next day, full of beans, he acted as if nothing had happened, a typical response to all our arguments.

The aftermath of this fracas was complete calmness. For once, my mother had been eclipsed. It seemed to perk her up, which made my father visibly relieved. But to this day, it still makes me feel guilty in the pit of my stomach.

She never contemplated stopping drinking though, and nor did I. We just brushed everything under the carpet and carried on. We were so similar in that respect.

In the middle of all of this, my younger sister, who was still living at home in my parents' little two-bedroom flat, teetotal and unable to get away from the daily drinking and arguing and shouting around her, started to break down mentally, hearing voices and locking herself in her room for hours. Her decline was rapid, and she went into a psychiatric ward where antipsychotic drugs were prescribed. After several weeks of terrible side effects from these drugs, she collapsed one night from heart failure. She was 25 years old when she died.

My mother's agony was complete. She had nothing to live for now.

She fell out with neighbours and rang doorbells to have it out with them, usually at night. They called the police. Once, she was arrested and her GP was informed. Her response was to bang on their doors again. She was outraged that anyone would call the police out on someone in such distress as hers. To her thinking, it showed how much they must hate her, which I think spurred her on. She was threatened with sectioning, and when she ignored the threats, she ended up in a psychiatric ward herself where she remained for two weeks. With immense shrewdness and lots of self-control, she cleaned up her act and behaved impeccably and compliantly while in the hospital. She was allowed to leave after several tests and group interviews, but on the recommendation that she partake in various group activities organised by the council, all of which she joined in with.

She was also a bit more careful with the neighbours after this. Where her family was concerned though, she went straight back to how she had been before with drinking and phoning family and various friends. This pattern of drinking and rowing and phoning happened over a period of 25 years, during which time my mother became more and more isolated, further estranged and racked with guilt.

Then one day in her mid-70s, she stopped drinking. And that was that. I suspect it had a lot to do with her diminishing mental agility at 75. She stopped interpreting comments negatively in the way she had always done in the past and started to take comments on face value.

This didn't happen overnight, but now when she had a few drinks, usually after a row with my father, she didn't go looking for answers to misunderstood comments of mine or my older sister's or anyone else's. The slowing mental pathways in her brain had stopped her thinking negatively at all. I know she found it quite hard to quit alcohol completely, but she had no use for it anymore.

But she did feel a lot of guilt for her phone calls to me and my sister over the years. Her way of dealing with it was to be as little a burden as possible on all around her. I think she felt she had been responsible for all bad things that had happened in the family, however big or small.

In Alcoholics Anonymous (AA) meetings, I have heard many people talk about the strange dichotomy between their low self-esteem and inflated ego. It seems to be an alcoholic thing. My mother felt overwhelmed by the inner belief that her merest presence was a burden to others. She was willing to observe but not participate. It was too painful for her.

Over the many years of our drinking together, there were – from my perspective – a few consolations that came out of it. Firstly, my mother, with a few exceptions, always seemed to behave worse than me. That was very comforting. It's maybe why I don't feel as guilty as I should do about my own behaviour.

Secondly, she made my own drinking feel perfectly normal. Alcohol was always a perfectly legitimate excuse for bad behaviour. I was never blamed by her for being drunk. That was unthinkable in her eyes.

Thirdly, when I got drunk and shouted at her, it made her feel better about her own behaviour. The angrier

I was to her, the better it made her feel about herself when we made up the next day – which we always did. I made her feel she wasn't alone disgracing herself. It was a bond we had, and it kept us on the same side, despite the shouting matches.

My mother and I did a lot of arguing over the years. The arguments always started when my mother got the merest inkling that I wasn't fully on her side in this whole ghastly family saga. She would then confidently tell me in what ways I was against her. Everything would escalate from there. They always started in this same way. We always made up in the end before the next drunken outburst. Our fighting was intense though, and we said some terrible things to each other. I wished her dead many times and swore at her. I even spat on her.

One Christmas Day, a friend of mine phoned me at my parents' flat with Christmas greetings. My mother answered and told him to fuck off and put the phone down. We were in the middle of a Christmas row. It was typical of how alcohol made her act. She felt the world was against her and struck out accordingly. It was instinctive and in keeping with how she reacted to everyone when she was drunk. She believed everyone was against her, and alcohol made her act on that belief.

The intensity of our fights was gruelling, flaring up, dying down, and flaring up again like forest fires. They could last days if insufficient time was left to sober us up properly.

I was ashamed of and embarrassed by her. She was affronted by my smugness, infuriated by what she saw as my aloofness to her situation.

When drunk, she didn't understand how much I believed in her, how strongly I believed her cause. She attacked me because of her own self-doubt; she believed she knew all my motives towards her, and alcohol made her fearless to speak out, and it made her feel better when she'd gone too far.

I drank as heavily as she did, always taking her drunkenness as a cue to my own. Neither of us ever made an attempt to stop or even to cut down during that time. Not in 25 years. Indeed, I felt I had no incentive to stop while my mother drank and dialled.

I was capable of behaving in much the same way as my mother, although at the time I didn't realise it. When I fell out with my own beloved friends on occasion, I would turn sarcastic and defensive through alcohol. I became paranoid and vocalised all my grievances. And I expected to be forgiven afterwards and my behaviour forgotten without fuss. It was a terrible blow when this didn't happen immediately. Not in the way that it did with my mother. I objected to being disapproved of. It's what led me back to the bottle the next day, to try and feel better about myself. I didn't repeat such episodes serially in the way my mother did, but in other circumstances, with less supportive friends around me, I might have done.

The arguments with my mother ceased when she gave up alcohol. Later, when I did the same, we had a few years to enjoy her sobriety, which I loved, and I was able to tell her what a kindred spirit she had been to me, aside from all the arguments, and how supportive she had been to me whenever I needed it. But she was full of guilt and inner remorse, which of course she struggled to talk in any detail about. By the time I stopped drinking, it was too late. I was losing her gradually to old age. She died last year.

I have tried to put all this to the back of my mind. Much of it was behind closed doors which seemed to diminish the need to address it. Besides, I felt I had made my peace with Mum in her sober years. But it says a lot about my drinking. In all this chaos, why did I drink? It inflamed every row. And yet in every row I drank. Where was my judgement?

In truth, I was never going to stop drinking as long as my mother drank too and accused me of disloyalty. I didn't want to stop drinking, and in the circumstances, I didn't see why I should. So, for 25 years, I fanned the flames by equalling my mother, drink for drink, and more.

In the end, I have to take responsibility for my part in the family meltdown, but the fact is while I was willing to do anything I could to make things better, I was not prepared to not drink.

Where did all this leave my relationship with alcohol? I was able to drink – for the greater part – without arguing amongst my own friends, so I felt I didn't have a problem, not like my mother. Even in the case of my mother, I didn't at the time think she had a serious alcohol problem. It was just that circumstances had driven her to drink, both of which she handled quite badly.

Alcoholics were very different sorts of people to me and my mother. Neither of us was physically dependent on alcohol, so we never thought we had a problem. The way we drank was our own choice, and we were prepared to take the consequences of that. Those consequences clearly never outweighed whatever it was that alcohol was doing for us. We were in control and acting from choice. That's not alcoholic... is it?

CHAPTER TWO

My Last Year of Drinking

I started what was to be my last year of drinking (assuming I never go back to it) in an unsettled state of mind and spirit. After four years in a loving relationship, I still hadn't been able to be honest with my partner, Jane, about my relationship with alcohol. I knew she thought I drank too much, but she didn't know the half of it. I had no desire to drink any less anyway. In fact, what I really wanted was more freedom to drink openly at weekends and in the evenings after work. Ideally, I wanted Jane to let her hair down a bit more and indulge with me in some spontaneous drinking when the urge took us. She enjoyed drinking, but only in order to get a bit tipsy, rarely drunk.

Jane was a firm believer in the buzz from the first drink, and would wait for exactly the right moment to indulge the buzz, knowing that once it had happened it wouldn't be enjoyed a second time. Not until the next social occasion anyway.

For me, the buzz needed chasing. And if Jane didn't want to keep chasing it with me, then I wanted to be allowed to chase it myself, without question or reproach. I wanted to be more honest about my love of alcohol.

My unsettled state, however, lay in knowing that any such hope of honesty on my part had long since evaporated. I had already lost my temper and turned sarcastic and vitriolic during too many drinking sessions to make it realistic to expect a more laissez faire attitude towards my drinking. I had been helplessly drunk at the end of too many nights out for Jane to think it was remotely sensible for me to drink more than I already did. I knew this without having to discuss it with Jane, so I didn't discuss it at all. Furthermore, if I had started on a campaign to allow more alcohol into my life, this would very probably have initiated the break-up of our relationship. We didn't share my love of alcohol. And so we couldn't all three be content together. I really didn't want to lose either of my life's passions, so I forced my drinking underground in order to keep the three of us happy.

This was a short-term solution at best. Secret drinking isn't easy to keep up without ever being noticed and I just wasn't very good at it. I would slur or stagger or lose my temper unexpectedly. I would appear drunk on my third glass of wine due to some earlier, secretive drinking, but absolutely fine the next occasion after a bottle. My drinking was getting more noticeably the central axis in all planned entertainment. There never seemed to be any social event that didn't involve alcohol. It was very obvious that the common denominator in my life was wine. But if that was becoming ever more predictable, my behaviour was not. It was only a matter of time before my alcoholic intake would become a matter for a serious discussion between Jane and I.

Instead of getting things onto my own terms by discussing my drinking before it became too much of an issue, I buried my head in the sand and hoped nothing would be said. I could have offered to stay sober on certain occasions or particular days in return for some open drinking when it would otherwise be frowned upon, like Saturday afternoons. I could have discussed my mood swings and allayed all fear by airing my self-doubts and inadequacies when calm and rational, instead of when fired up, drunk, and angry.

Then I had a particularly big binge. It started on a Saturday at lunchtime with a BBQ, after which we all went off to watch a local football match. There was a bar, and after the match, we went on to a local pub where some more friends joined us. Then finally we went for a curry. I downed alcohol at every opportunity. I drank and drank and drank, laughed and cried and laughed again and fell asleep at the restaurant table. Then Jane walked me home and returned to the restaurant. The following morning, I awoke, confronted with the conversation I dreaded more than any other. It started with, "I think we need to talk about your drinking."

I hurriedly pieced together the events of the previous day while lying there in bed on Sunday morning, cringing at various snatches of memory: crying about my late sister in the pub, falling asleep after the poppadums in the curry house. Was it possible nobody had noticed, including Jane? No. It was she who had propelled me home early and gone back to the restaurant on her own. Then I remembered I'd phoned her an hour later, still very drunk of course, thinking it was 3:30am. To the hilarity of the group back in the restaurant, she corrected my mistake over the phone. "It's nine o'clock in the evening. Are you upside down?" she asked.

It felt humiliating because I had been too drunk to conceal anything from anyone. I was so disappointed that I had allowed myself to get into such a vulnerable state – out of control, unable to behave normally in public, all thanks to my much greater than usual intake of booze. There were pluses, however. Clearly, I had not got into an argument with anyone or turned sarcastic in my drunken state. And it seemed everyone thought the call to Jane in the restaurant was very funny. So, I had entertained the group. This was surely a drinking anecdote that could be recounted fondly for some time to come.

Nonetheless, it was an unforgiveable mistake and gave Jane the perfect opportunity to confront my drinking head on. I had nothing in my defence. And I surrendered.

Maybe it was surrendering that triggered the sudden and profound change of desire in me. I had done so in the instant because I felt defeated by the obvious truth about my excessive drinking and the best way to rectify the situation was not to tackle Jane but to accept the charge and tackle the excessive drinking head on.

I pledged to cut back right away, and as I did, I realised that what I was saying was the absolute truth. The switch within me had already happened such that the words uttered from my mouth were playing catch up with what had already occurred.

Looking back on this incident now, I don't really know how I was able to be so convinced. It must have been something to do with the change of desire in me, triggered by my acceptance of the situation I found myself in, with nowhere to hide.

I couldn't wait to get going, demonstrate to her and, most importantly, to myself that I could stop after one glass of wine. I was sure that I could do it. Not only could I stop drinking after one glass, I could stop wanting any more wine after that one glass. I felt that I could somehow set a ceiling on my desire as well as my consumption.

And from that day forward, I went at it with zeal.

Once I realised it was possible to drink moderately, I was brimming with eagerness to experience what life was like for the moderate drinker. To carry on the way moderates did. One glass at home, then up to, but no more than, two glasses on the weekend. The desire miraculously switched off at two glasses. A whole new world appeared to open up. It was as if I had walked through a door to a new society I didn't previously know existed.

I set a limit of no more than half a bottle of wine on any occasion – ever. There was simply no need for any more than that. I would aim to drink no more than one (largish) glass of wine per night but build in at least two alcohol-free nights per week.

To keep it all manageable, I would stick to wine only (no other alcoholic beverages), and I would drive to social occasions and stay within the legal limit. This would help to keep me on the straight and narrow, providing extra incentive towards moderation, and was a great demonstration to Jane that I was taking things seriously.

It worked. All of it. I enjoyed the one glass of wine with dinner, swilling it around my mouth before swallowing, and really savouring every moment. This was after all what wine was famed for – its compliment to food. The French only ever drank wine with steak or cheese, didn't they? I was able to stick to the limits I had set with ease.

When we went on holiday to Portugal, I stayed away from the bar at the airport – that was a bit harder – and I drove our hire car every night to the restaurants of Sagres and kept within my parameters – no more than half a bottle. Even when we left the car back at the apartment, I stuck to the rules. It was not only easy, but enjoyable.

I succeeded in keeping the new regime up for several weeks, eight or nine in fact. I felt as though I had cracked it. I truly believed I didn't want to get drunk anymore. And the proof of the pudding lay in the drinking. I drank moderately and enjoyed every moment, stopping every time after reaching my set limit.

It is very hard to convey what a sense of achievement this was and how happy it made me. I listened to warnings on the radio about new evidence of excessive drinking and I thought, I'm okay. I don't need to turn the radio off mid-report for fear of hearing things I didn't want to face up to. I had nothing to hide from anymore. As a bonus, I felt fit and healthy too. No more hangovers. I wondered why I had never tried this before and why I had worried about having a drink problem.

In fairness to the facts though, I didn't go to the pub with boozy mates during this time, and the one big social event I attended was with Jane and we took the car, which I drove, so there was no opportunity to get drunk. As a result, temptation was removed. I was fine all evening, although I did get a bit bored after the food was cleared away and I had consumed my quotient of wine. But I still wasn't tempted to break the rules.

My desire not to get drunk outweighed all other emotions. Besides I was still able to enjoy a glass or two of red wine, and for that I was truly grateful.

For the next few weeks, I socialised very little, out of temptation's way, and I was absolutely fine with my wine rationing and my alcohol-free nights at home.

Then a friend told me he had got me a Glastonbury ticket, and a switch, the desire-switch in my head that had been turned off when I pledged to slow down my drinking, somehow got switched back on again without my knowing.

I didn't change any of the new rules, which I continued to stick to rigidly, but I did plan to relax the rules while at the festival and then go back the regime once I came back.

As the festival got nearer and nearer, the anticipation and excitement grew. Of course it would, the desire switch had been turned back on. I was now sticking to the drinking rules only with great determination and will-power. The level of restraint required was huge.

My excitement in the 24 hours before setting off was intense and all bottled up. We had an epic journey planned to the West Country via Birmingham involving an overnight stay, a hire-car, and a coach. And we drank at every opportunity. My festival supply of booze was out by the time we arrived at the site. It didn't matter. Alcohol was everywhere.

I could feel the old me taking over the controls, and for six days, I drank all day and into the evening, and I loved every moment of it. I convinced myself that I would address my drinking when I got home, so there was no need to worry now. So, I didn't.

At the end of the festival, we joined the multitudes waiting for trains home in the sweltering heat. On the platform of the local station, exhausted revellers lay sprawled against rucksacks feebly clutching their bottles of water. I, however, was frantically scurrying around looking for licensed premises where I could buy more hooch. Incredibly, there was no pub at or near the station – I searched high and low for one – and no off licences either. But as we had planned to break the journey home for a last night of freedom, it wasn't long before I was back in a pub and then a curry house, and on the party went in my head. I couldn't bear the thought of it coming to an end. I just had to keep it going.

We had managed to eke one last day and night out of the trip but now we were on the final final leg home – the train journey back to London. Depression had set in. I knew I had to turn the alcohol desire switch off again in my head, but I had no means of finding it. The time had come to go back to the rule book, but I had no desire for sobriety. I bought 2 cans of Strongbow from the train's buffet trolley in defiance of the situation, to try and give myself a little buzz. I buried all thoughts of what I had pledged to do on return from the festival.

Back home I knew I had to appear to be in control of my drinking, but instantly it was a struggle. The rule was one glass per day, which was going to take all the will-power I had – which was nowhere near enough. I reassured myself that I could openly pour two biggish glasses without causing Jane too much concern, but that still wasn't enough to satisfy my need.

So I went back to buying vodka for the journey home from work on the train and sneaking shots of spirits at home. There was no chance of pouring a gin and tonic before dinner without drawing attention to my gradually increasing drinking. So, it went underground.

For the next few months, I drank publicly at the 'one-glass – no-more-than half-a-bottle' rate, and secretly with whatever I could get away with and still appear sober.

On the surface, it worked. Underneath, I was jumpy, frustrated, and missing something. The old voice in my head was telling me: if something is enjoyable, then it will be many times more enjoyable after a few drinks.

Before Glastonbury, my settings were stable at the lower rate of alcohol intake. I had successfully got them down to a sensible level and had acclimatised myself to them immediately, and I had been enjoying my new life as a moderate drinker.

After Glastonbury, I couldn't go back to those levels without a mental battle. I couldn't just switch from one mode to another. I didn't know what the trigger was that allowed me to reset the boundaries. Something had to happen, an event of some kind, a shake-up. I really didn't know what though.

When I pledged to cut down my intake all those months earlier, my desire to do so was strong enough to make it possible. But once that desire for moderation was lost, after Glastonbury festival, I had no idea how to get it back again.

Then, towards the end of the year, two things happened that would change everything once more.

I got drunk and allowed my paranoia about Jane's disapproval of me over some matter to come out in a rage. We had friends over for dinner that night. There was wine, of course. Lots of it in my case. I felt resentful and it all came out. I told Jane's friends to leave the house, and I tore into Jane verbally as soon as they were out the door. On and on I went, fuelled by paranoia, wine, and the absolute belief I was right about her disapproval of me. I stormed out of the house slamming the front door. I dread to think what was going through her head when she realised that the old me had woken up from his slumber.

As I sat with my head in my hands on someone's front garden wall, the quiet after the storm, my own storm, I wondered how I had let any of it happen. I knew that the alcohol had ignited my temper, and once again I had created misery for everyone including myself.

The next day, I slunk off to work and snuck a couple of miniature vodkas early to steady myself and to hide from the reality of what I had done. I apologised in my time-honoured, vodka-fuelled way, and in so doing I bought myself a little grace.

A few days later, when the dust had settled from this incident, I realised how inevitable it was that things would go wrong again. Where or how, I couldn't predict.

Sure enough, within only a few weeks I would do it again, in a more public place this time. Not with Jane, but with my bosses, in front of my colleagues. Now, despite my secret drinking at work, I was not prepared to take big risks with my job. I did the drinking thing at work with the sure knowledge that I would get away with it. For this reason, I was always nervous of work parties because I felt there was a risk I would get drunk and say something stupid. I generally had to prepare mentally before work's Christmas and summer socials, even at Friday night drinks to celebrate the end of the week.

On this occasion, a mere two weeks after the outburst with Jane, I had taken myself off to the pub at lunchtime, nothing unusual about that, and had anticipated my own mental state ahead of a big night out with bosses and colleagues which had been planned in advance to celebrate some sort of group achievement. (There was no prospect in my mind of not drinking at this celebration, by the way.)

We reached the bar at about 6 p.m. and spirits were high as the first drinks were eagerly consumed by my colleagues and bosses. Then we went for dinner and there were bottles of wine on the table, but not everyone was drinking. I poured wine for anyone who would accept my advances with red and white in each hand, which I then placed within easy reach of me. Over dinner, I got into a discussion with one of the senior management team who was being a bit smug in my opinion. I felt myself get belligerent, but I overrode the warning light in my brain that said, "Leave it alone, talk to someone else." He had said something that was inconsistent and which disproved his whole point.

I was delighted. I wouldn't let it go, and I thought I was being very clever in bringing him back to his error at every opportunity, glugging wine as I went, shutting out everything else around me so I could concentrate on fixing this dude in a verbal headlock. That was until I noticed people starting to leave the restaurant. We had finished the meal, to be fair, so it was a suitable time to go, but it was obvious they weren't hanging around. They'd had enough. A sickness in my stomach made me aware that I had upset these people somehow, not so much in what I had said but with my aggressive attitude, and I really wanted a last chance to show them that it was all fine and we were having fun. But it was too late. People clearly weren't having fun and thought it best to leave before an argument developed. I yearned inside to tell them that there would be no argument, but they were off, and others followed them. I went home with a supply of vodka, enough to blot everything out.

The aftermath was painful and undignified. I was profuse and gallant in my apology and was so willing to take whatever punishment awaited me that they were happy to forgive me. It wasn't the drink that bothered them so much as the revelation of a deep dissatisfaction, one that I had been unable to share with them before. What they couldn't understand was why had I never mentioned the thing that was troubling me at a more appropriate time, like a Monday morning meeting? The reality was that this issue didn't really bother me that much when I was sober. But after a few drinks I felt empowered to let rip.

For now, having swallowed a big, choking mouthful of the richest humble pie, washed down with a jug of humiliation, I had got away with it. And it was December. Party season. I had survived the work scare, the slate was clean at home, and the drink was flowing. I could relax and enjoy life once again.

Well, almost. I knew that I was on a last chance. I felt the thinness of the ice beneath me and the anticipation from all quarters of what might happen the next time. Would there be a next time? Of course there would. Somehow, I had to live with what I had created for myself and hope that there was enough trust left in me to keep my relationship and my job in place.

I figured that the best way to demonstrate to all those around me that I was doing something about my alcohol consumption was to embark on a dry January. I knew I was capable of it, having four years ago achieved almost a whole one.

It was a no-brainer. There was little more than 10 days to Christmas; I could surely keep my behaviour in check, drunk or not, until after the holiday shutdown was over, whilst mentally preparing for a dry January. I felt relieved that I was facing my demons again, and I still had a few more days to enjoy before the self-imposed prohibition kicked in.

The desire for sobriety was possibly coming back! By the end of January, I might be ready once again to embrace moderation, just as I had done earlier in the year when I cut down.

But there was a problem. It was my 50th birthday in the middle of January. I couldn't be sober at my own birthday party in front of all my drinking friends. That was unthinkable in terms of my own enjoyment of such a big occasion, and besides I doubted my friends would ever forgive me if I drank water or Coke on my birthday. I also realised that if I had an alcohol binge in the middle of January, then there was little prospect of returning to moderate consumption for the remainder of the month. My pre- and post-Glastonbury festival experiences were proof of this, if it was needed. Once I had turned to heavy drinking, there was a very real danger that the switch would get jammed and it might be months or years before I was ready to switch it off again.

Then the thought occurred to me: how much easier life would be if alcohol was removed from the picture completely. I didn't see this as a solution to my immediate dilemma, it was merely a fantasy in which all these complications would disappear. I was indulging a daydream. I pictured myself chatting away with friends as they got drunker and drunker and I poured wine into people's glasses as I went around my groups of friends in total control. I even imagined getting into my car and driving home with Jane, dropping various friends off en route. I realised that some people did actually do that sort of thing all the time. The mere thought of it came across as uber cool.

I half wondered if it were possible and then dismissed the idea as ridiculous. But the seed was sown.

The options whirled around in my head as I imagined being dry for two weeks, then celebrating my birthday for the night and going back to being dry for the next two weeks. The more I toyed with this idea, the more unrealistic it seemed. The only possibility seemed to be to cancel the birthday celebrations and go through with the dry January.

Then I thought again about my 50th party, and all the other big ones before it, my 40th my 30th and even as far back as my 20th, and I thought about some of the big ones in between, and they all had the same chaotic drunken forgetfulness in common, the feeling of regret the next day, regret for my behaviour, for neglecting certain guests, for not thanking people for their generosity, for forgetting huge chunks of the night, including how I had got home. It led me to question whether I really wanted to go through that again. I mean, I was prepared to do it, of course, but did I really want it? Didn't I want to do things differently if I possibly could? By questioning my desire for drink, I realised that something was happening that I had never really thought seriously about before. At all times up until now, my desire for alcohol was as strong as my desire to stay alive. Now, I felt that perhaps it wasn't as strong as that. And if it wasn't that strong, then maybe some of these other ways of doing things – like staying sober and chatting to everyone, making sure they were looked after, catching up with their news and then driving home – were all possibilities too.

I had never even considered such a thing before, let alone actually done it. I could reinvent myself. I could turn myself from being this dependent drinker, on the edge, into the very opposite. I thought about famous people I admired who didn't need to drink anymore and were able to entertain others on an epic scale without alcohol – Frank Skinner, Billy Connolly, Ruby Wax. I imagined I was able to enjoy myself in the same way as them – minus the comic routine, wit, glamorous lifestyle, and money. And I wondered if I had something inside me that alcohol was holding back. I entertained the idea that maybe I could do great things if I allowed myself the freedom. I started to think that I might have a choice.

For the next few days, I carried on in much the same vein as in previous Decembers, but this time, with every mouthful of alcohol, I really thought about what I was doing to myself and why. I realised how bored I was of the routine. The booze wasn't really having much effect anymore anyway. It was helping me get through the day sometimes, but I wasn't excited or happy at the prospect of drinking it. I was so used to its effects that I drank it on auto-pilot and felt nothing special at all – just the same as every other day. The time of year made booze so readily available, it all seemed very predictable. I felt I had really done the whole drinking thing to the absolute limit and back, and that now I was just going round and round the same circuit. I had got absolutely the most from it for 36 years, and if I really wanted a new adventure, it would need to be a completely different one. The world of sobriety could surely be made fun with a bit of effort, and I felt ready to make that effort. Part of the fun was that I had no idea where this adventure would take me, but I knew that what I was getting excited about was the feeling of liberty.

So, all of a sudden, three themes were running through my brain, not all of them entirely positive. The first was the boredom with the old way of doing things; the second was the reinvention of myself into something brand new, and the third was the fear of the complete unknown. Maybe I had got it all wrong, and I would miss drinking; my mates would all think I was too dull, as would I, and I would get straight back on the alcohol with renewed vigour!

But there was surely a brand-new adventure to be had, one that might be worth embarking on. Weirdly, the idea of the alcohol-free world was so alien to me that I saw sobriety as a kind of narcotic. You would "take sobriety" and find yourself with heightened awareness – one that enabled you to really understand what people were saying to you all evening and you could answer them intelligently and sometimes mildly amusingly. That's what I'd seen other people do on this drug, and I wanted to be like them for a change. They actually seemed pretty cool to me for the first time. Then again, maybe they were having a terrible trip and were longing like me, to be gloriously drunk. It seemed unlikely. Sober people always seemed very self-contained.

I reminded myself of the dry January from four years previous. I quite enjoyed the world as seen from the sober side, but the difference was that during that dry January, I didn't belong in the sober world, I was 'just visiting.' My mind-set was still with the drinkers and my identity too – I made sure the company I was with was aware of my temporary affliction for which I received sympathy and admiration.

Stopping drinking altogether required a different language and culture, neither of which I knew at all. It was a whole new world.

I felt exhilarated at my new idea and figured that soon I would be ready to experiment with the new drug. Seeing sobriety in this way helped me get psyched up and enthused for stopping. I didn't want to change my friends or stop seeing people in certain places, such as restaurants or bars and pubs; I wanted to keep my social life more or less the same as in my drinking days only from now on it would be on my new 'drink' of choice – the sobriety drug that would empower me to do everything I wanted.

If the whole thing was intolerably dull, then I would just have to find new ways to amuse myself – I made that a promise to myself, but the option to go back to drinking wasn't an option anymore. I had done the drinking thing and was bored with it. Time to move on!

I had some hurdles to get over first though. The biggest one was telling people my idea. I hadn't discussed it with anyone so far. I wondered whether revealing it might alter my perception dramatically. I might for instance come to my senses at the first note of incredulity from Jane or close friends. I might realise instantly what an idiot I had been and change my mind again.

I figured that some friends might be disappointed in me when they heard my plan – they might tell me I didn't need to give up booze, that I was such a laugh when I'd had a few drinks it would be such a shame to stop. And maybe on hearing this, I might agree with them and pledge to carry on exactly as before.

If I decided to go through with the plan (and at this point I wasn't 100% sure that I would), it was imperative to tell Jane about my intentions in time for her to adjust to the idea. She would be the most affected by my sobriety, in good and bad ways. For several years, I had put her through quite a lot of pain with my drinking, so I didn't want to get her hopes up falsely by pledging to stop and then changing my mind. On the other hand, I knew it would be strange for her to be the sole drinker in our partnership, and I didn't know how she would feel about that. I needed to give her plenty of warning. But I had to be sure of my decision first.

I really dithered over when to tell her. In the end, I just blurted it out as an unplanned announcement, not only to Jane but to a group of close friends at yet another boozy pre-Christmas meal. After several glasses of red wine, I told the group around the table that I was going to stop drinking altogether in the New Year. I even told them I was going to attend AA meetings – more for effect, as I really wanted to make a statement that would be hard for me to go back on without losing a bit of face. I was slightly scared that I might capitulate if anyone started saying I was being ridiculous and didn't need to stop. The AA bit served to harden my resolve all the more, as well as putting off anyone from dissuading me.

So, I had made my announcement, and like the wedding banns, I awaited any objections, of which of course there were none. I realise now that no one really believed me, they just thought it was another of my drunken outpourings.

It was up to me when, where, and how I made it all happen.

How do you decide such a thing? I knew for sure that I wanted it to be when I was ready, not on some arbitrary date such as New Year's Eve. So, I thought it would be sensible to make the launch sometime between Christmas and New Year's without deciding the actual day until closer to the time and without making any further announcements in case I wanted to change the date for any reason. I knew I wanted to go through with it, but I wanted to make sure I did it on the best footing, which meant giving myself some flexibility if needed.

Christmas and Boxing Day came and went. I drank wine without enthusiasm, but I didn't hold back either. I wanted to concentrate on just how pointless an activity drinking really is. I wanted to focus on how unnecessary it is to the enjoyment of the occasion. When I went to work on the day after Boxing Day, a Friday, I decided that morning to make that the last day of drinking. It felt right. Jane was away with her family and due back home the next day. I was seeing some old friends that night for dinner, and I figured this would be the night of my final drink.

All day, I mused on my future life as a teetotaller, focussing principally on the positives – the freedom I believed it would give me, the freedom from all those worries about alcohol. I had a few drinks during the day, as usual, and when I bought some wine for my last night of drinking, it was unceremonious and I was unmoved emotionally. I knew exactly what each glass of wine would do to me, how it would make me feel, and how much more of it I was likely to drink, knowing it was my last night. I really believed that my 36-year friendship with booze was at an end and this was our last night together. I had no regrets and no sentimentality. And so it was. Another night on the wine and spirits, a staggered journey home on the train and bus, and a collapse into bed. I didn't need to kid myself anymore about how much or little I had actually consumed, how well or badly I had behaved, or how loud and opinionated I had been with my friends. I could let it all go.

CHAPTER THREE

Stopping Drinking

**Day One. The Day After
My Final Night of Drinking.**

Saturday. I awoke without any immediate recollection of going to bed the night before and with a strong sense that today was important, in a gloomy sort of way. Then things started flashing into my mind, like saying goodbye to my friends and laughing and hugging and promising to meet again soon. But I knew that something needed resolving....

Then I remembered what it was. I'd stopped drinking. That's what was causing the anxiety. I had a sick feeling in the pit of my stomach as the weary realisation came over me that things were going to be very difficult today. Right at that moment, as things stood, I had had my last drink, according to the plan.

Then a tiny flash of hope lifted me for a second when I thought how easy it would be to not tell anyone what I had done and just carry on with my drinking for another day. Nobody needed know anything about last night. Jane was returning home after spending Christmas with her parents that day, so I had another 24 hours if I wanted it. I could treat last night as a practice run for what it would feel like when I did actually stop. But for now, however, I could just carry on drinking if I wanted to. I had the option at any time.

I went out to buy some milk and found my eyes seeking out the section in the shop fridge where the cans of spirit mixers were. It would have been so easy to buy two of these for later that day. Although the urge to do this was strong, I ignored it. And again, on the way back from the shop, passing the pub, it appeared people had started to get into the weekend vibe already, quenching their thirst, probably with cold cider or maybe a few pints of Kronenburg.

I yearned to go in and join them, but my legs kept moving in the direction of home. I became instantly aware of the conflicting forces within me. I absolutely wanted a drink and I absolutely wouldn't allow myself to have one. It was a stalemate. I needed to put it out of my mind and get on with something else, but I kept being reminded of alcohol. It seemed to be everywhere.

I figured the best thing to do would be to drive to Gatwick to pick up Jane. That way, I knew I wouldn't reach for a drink, not at least before the car was out of my hands. I could tell her about my decision to stop drinking on our drive back home, and once I'd told her, I would feel stronger about my commitment. I would be sure to stop wavering. So, I texted her and we sorted out a meeting point. Now, I could relax a bit. I would be driving shortly, so I had no reason to be tempted by alcohol.

I set off for the airport at dusk. It was all very Christmassy and my head filled with thoughts of mulled wine and whisky Macs and how I was missing them. How I was never going to be having them again. This was the worst time in the day to be reminded of alcohol, especially since the effects of last night's intake were still with me and begging to be topped up.

And then, as if the God of Temptation were out to test me to the limit, my car broke down and I came to a halt next to a bar-restaurant just south of Croydon. In spite of its location, this hostelry was quite simply the most inviting-looking place I could ever have imagined on a dark, cold, blustery December evening. I figured that now I could have a drink while I waited for the car recovery man to arrive. I could sit at the bar and look out of the window directly at my knackered old banger. My old car had delivered me one last act of perfect loyalty. It had sacrificed itself for me in such a way as I could pay homage to it as I looked on from my bar stool and said thank you.

I texted Jane to explain what had happened and to suggest she make her own way home while I sorted the car out.

I sat inside my loyal old banger and waited. The bar had its Christmas decorations up and all the bottles and glasses were gleaming in the seductive low-level lighting. Tempting as it was, I just couldn't bring myself to go in there though. I knew I had more fight in me than that, and I was both relieved and disappointed at the same time. After an hour of solitude, the vehicle rescue man arrived to free me from my hell.

At the time, I didn't realise it, but that early evening in Croydon, sitting in my car outside the bar waiting for the recovery services to arrive was the closest thing to temptation that I was ever going to get. I had only stopped drinking for half a day.

Perhaps if I had known it was never again going to be as tempting as that, I would have felt more empowered to get through the next 12 hours of sobriety. But I didn't, and I still clutched at the thought that until I told someone I had stopped drinking, then I was technically at liberty to carry on.

So, I sat there in silent thought, fearing that it would all go on being as awful as this for days, even weeks. I just needed to declare my decision so that I didn't keep wavering. I needed to tell Jane.

It was another awful moment when I announced it to her, like telling someone some terrible news, except the news was terrible for me. My reaction at delivering the news was the same as if I had just received it. I felt devastated and trapped. But not tempted. I was going to have to learn how to do things differently.

Alcohol would never again present itself as a real option – a proper choice. Sure, the first evening everything felt flat, dull, and depressing. The mere thought of dinner without wine on the table made me feel as though I had made a big mistake. No longer did I need to think of spurious celebrations in order that Cava or Prosecco could be opened or sudden feelings of depression to excuse the gin being poured before dinner.

But as flat as all this felt, it wasn't will-power that was getting me through it. I had no desire for alcohol even though I knew it was missing. My desire was for sobriety. But this was a new world with different feelings and desires, ups and downs – all of which I had to get acquainted with.

I would have to learn to enjoy meals all over again and with a whole new set of desires, dinner in particular. But for now, day one was through. I had my first sober day under my belt. I lay in bed that night glowing with pride but thinking I would be awake all night. Instead, I was asleep in seconds.

Day Two. My first AA meeting

That night, I slept badly and awoke drenched in sweat. I had a slightly nauseous feeling, but I felt alive. Very pleasingly, every mouthful of water, tea, or coffee was restorative and invigorating. I came to life with simple stimulants. Food didn't tire me out instantly or leave me sprawled in front of the telly for hours on end. On the contrary, each mouthful gave me a little more energy. This was a miracle as far as I was concerned, and never a feature of any of my former hangovers.

I felt part of something now. I had gone a whole day without alcohol, and however slight an achievement this was, it signalled that I was on the other side now.

I felt tired and energised at the same time. My brain was telling me I had not slept a full night and that I needed to close my eyes and get some more rest, but my body felt as light as a feather and able to respond to the commands I gave it. Simple tasks like checking if the phone was charged or reaching for a glass of water required no effort. Gone was the lethargic clumsiness of my usual hangover.

I was also able to recall every moment of the evening before, however trivial the thing, and so there was no need for angst or anguish or embarrassment of any kind.

This was a big day as I had planned to attend my first AA meeting. AA was not something I felt in desperate need of, but I knew I had done something special, and I wanted to give myself some recognition for that. AA was the only thing I could think of that would provide it. In honesty I had no idea what to expect, and I felt a little nervous.

I felt that AA would consummate my decision to not drink. I believed I would come out on the other side of the meeting as a different person.
The problem was that I had heard AA was a quasi-religious organisation, and I really didn't want anything that involved praying or holding hands.

When I arrived at the large church hall, I expected to see tramps in macs, unshaven and unclean, hanging about looking furtive. Instead, I saw gregarious smokers around the entrance to the hall and tried to figure out what that signified. As I made my way into the hall I was convinced everyone would be looking at me. They weren't of course; they were chatting away, drinking coffee and acting perfectly normally, or they were sitting quietly waiting for the meeting to commence. Within moments we were under way. I heard people share their feelings and experiences and a growing niggling doubt came over me that perhaps I had overreacted to my "problem" by stopping altogether. I felt that in all probability I was just weak and undisciplined and perfectly capable of pulling my socks up.

I felt like a bit of an imposter, as if I had turned up on the infectious diseases ward of a busy hospital with nothing more than a heavy cold. On the surface, I fitted in because I had decided to stop drinking. But I was asking myself whether I should really be here at all? Did I really share that much in common with these people and their tales of children taken into care, of attempts at suicide, or their long bouts in rehab? Had I taken the proverbial sledgehammer to crack a nut? I was within days of turning 50, almost a lifetime of comparatively trouble-free drinking behind me. Many of the people around me in this full-to-bursting church hall had been in their 20s when AA had saved them from certain death, so I was told.

Though I knew my drinking had got a bit out of hand and I needed to take a really good look at myself, I felt that I was nowhere near as bad as some of those around me in that AA meeting.

On the flip side, I feared that if I had another drink, I would simply carry on the way I had been doing for 36 years. I knew I didn't want that either.

I came out of the meeting and into the winter air with a sense of trepidation. I looked at the pub across the road. It was just the sort of place I would normally head for to celebrate an achievement, however small. I had a real urge to go in, but at the same time an absolute conviction that I wouldn't do so. I knew that this was a struggle that lay before me everywhere I went, but I knew also I wasn't alone. All of those people in the meeting had to pass the same pub every time they emerged from the church. I felt such warmth from that thought. The shared experience made a big difference. We had all done something amazing, and our meeting was a reminder to ourselves of that; in fact, it was a celebration of it. These people knew what a big thing it was to not drink, and if ever I wanted or needed comfort in that thought, they were always there to remind me.

Days 3 to 7

For the next few days, I thought about drinking even more than before. I became fascinated by other people's habits as I glimpsed them through restaurant windows or in bars as they nursed a glass of wine or beer. I would feel disappointed if they were drinking coffee or juice and would look for evidence their drinks were cocktails or their coffees liqueur-infused. Everyone seemed to be drinking so slowly. I wanted them to take the opportunities that I had now denied myself, and I felt some strong pangs for my drinking days, but nothing that I could call real temptation. There was no way I was going to change my decision. I had mixed feelings about that – relief that I was strong enough to continue, and heartbreak that I had lost my old way of life.

I can still have a pang or two every now and then. I liken it to looking at an old photo album, if ever I have a wave of nostalgia about my drinking days. I feel regret that it's all over, but do I want to go back there again? Not really.

Then, to make sure that my pang doesn't give way to temptation, I evoke my three core principles... one: I remind myself what a drink would lead to if I had one now. It wouldn't be just one drink. Even if it didn't all end up really badly, that one drink would set in motion a session dominated by booze. Two: I had done that sort of thing all my life and was tired of doing it over and over again. Three: Now I wanted control, freedom, and a different sort of adventure.

First Month

Around two weeks after quitting, I found that as each day wore on, I missed having a drink to look forward to when I got home after work and would need to recite my three core principles several times an hour from the moment I left my place of work. Yet though I definitely felt a sense of great loss I still wasn't tempted to take a drink. The first time I went back to a favourite pub, I looked around as though for a friend, one who I knew had been in there moments earlier. The moment passed, however, and I tried to focus on the things I was allowed to have in my new existence.
I quickly became dependent on certain comforts like coffee, Diet Coke, chewing gum, chocolate,

ice cream, and sparkling water. These weren't substitutes for alcohol. Not consciously anyway. I didn't think that sparkling water was like sparkling wine; it's just that if you want to treat yourself, and alcohol is not in any way an option, then you choose things that give you a lift. At the start, I had no idea what I liked or disliked or what gave me a lift because in my drinking days I only ever wanted alcohol. I knew what chocolate tasted like, but not how to enjoy it. I had to learn how to get the most pleasure from such luxuries, as though discovering them for the first time. I felt like a child again, giggling to myself as I munched a bar of chocolate at 9am.

Oddly, it was coffee that made me feel the most excited in those very early days, probably because out of all the pleasures I was relearning to enjoy, coffee was the nearest substitute for alcohol. Perhaps it was the buzz from the caffeine. I went to the cinema and theatre in the fortnight after giving up alcohol and found myself getting really excited about the prospect of drinking coffee on arrival. I even had a slight feeling of panic if coffee wasn't going to be served.

By direct contrast, tea made me deflated. Tea was the drink I should have been drinking when I elected to have alcohol. It had bad associations. If I'm honest, it still does. I don't think I'll ever get over that one.

But I discovered the biggest buzz from drinking

sparkling water, ice and lemon, out of a large wine glass when I went to restaurants, knowing that this delicious, refreshing drink was going to make me sharper and more energised as the night went on, like a new drug. I quickly realised that my classy new drink set me apart from everyone else. It was the cheapest drink on the table and I could order as much as I liked of it without ever worrying what it would do to my brain or my behaviour. Furthermore, at the end of the night, when I left the restaurant, I could get into my car, parked outside the restaurant, and drive home in complete control to awake the next day feeling amazing. It's horribly smug, I know. But God, I didn't care. It felt a million dollars. And the feeling hasn't worn off one tiny little bit.

How did I get through social events?

My 50th birthday party, three weeks after giving up alcohol, was a watershed. I had absolutely no doubt in my mind that I would get through the night without drinking, but I feared how much of an ordeal it would be. Driving to the central London venue on a Saturday night knowing that I would be driving home at the end was both exhilarating and depressing at the same time. But the prospect of all those people offering me drinks all night was nothing short of daunting. And what were we all going to talk about all night? I didn't really ever do social events sober. I had no idea what to expect.

In reality, it wasn't as hard as I had feared. Once

people understood that I had stopped drinking altogether, they were so shocked that they didn't know what to say. It was as though I had given them some awful news, or something. There wasn't a hint of persuasion from any of them.

I had to learn the hard way how parties are just an endless round of small talk as people get more and more pissed and emotional. I was gearing myself up for meeting with and talking in depth to all these people from my past, trying to remember the names of their children and all the big things in their lives, and I needn't have bothered because you get so little chance for any of that. Parties are all about surface chat and awkward pauses and excuses to move away.

I was exhausted by the end nonetheless. I could see in everyone's eyes, they were in their own worlds, and I could see the attraction of that. I could also observe the light drinkers amongst my friends. They seemed to be having a good time too, and when I talked to them, it was as if we were in our own club, the Wide-Awake Club. And I was fine with that. I drove home with Jane after what felt like an eternity, dropping one or two revellers on the way, and then we flopped into bed.

Jane had only a few glasses as per the norm on such occasions, and I could see how my former heavy drinking must have made her feel all those times coming home with a drunk deadweight. I think she too was in shock that night.

The next day, I had a headache and my brain felt like cotton wool. I wasn't supposed to feel like that after a night of sobriety. It was brain fatigue from all the concentration, which was something I would have to get used to after socialising. You can't just switch off.

I realised that I could get through any social occasion sober if I could get through my own 50th birthday party in a pub. But for the next few weeks, I would think about alcohol pretty much all of the time.

I was surprised to find that once in a social setting, my behaviour was much the same as before. I was talkative and quite loud at times, but I felt in much greater control of my behaviour and I knew when I had gone a bit far or if I needed to get more involved. I also knew when I'd had enough, and driving home with Jane was a joy. It still is.

But there were awkwardnesses too. When sober, you think about the conversation you are having, where it is going, how it will end, or how you will move on to a different topic, and that can be tiring. Two sober people talking together can get very intense because sometimes they don't know how to get out of what they're discussing or when to move away. Alcohol not only takes the edge off ones' anxieties, but it allows us to talk without thinking – and that can be very relaxing in itself. Drinkers don't care about the next conversation, just the current one, which is why they too can get intense, but not from a position of anxiety or else they just change the subject randomly. Being around drinkers can be more relaxing than around sober people because when drinkers let their hair down, they really relax. The moderates also seem to know when they've had enough to drink and are happy to stop at that point – not something I have much experience with.

But if at any moment I felt sad about my non-drinking status, the biggest motivator to keep sober was to remind myself...

You've done drinking to death.
There is nothing more you can get from it that you haven't tried a thousand and one times already.
It doesn't always work anyway.
Why not do something new that doesn't involve booze? Just give it a go.

Sobriety is a big deal. Everyone will be amazed if you stop drinking. But you know what? It's not as if you have to learn a whole new language or grade 8 piano. Anyone can desire language or intricate skills – that's the easy bit – it's the doing that's hard. But with cutting out alcohol, it's the other way around.

Finding the desire to not drink is the hard part. Once you've mastered that, everything else is much easier than it looks.

Have I Stopped Wanting to See My friends?

Perversely, I have really enjoyed meeting with my old drinking pals. I have insisted on one thing though – with varying degrees of success. That is food. I am delighted to spend a night out socialising in boozy company as long as there are plenty of treats and activities for me too. Yes, eating is an activity which helps to bring structure to the evening, some welcome landmarks to the entertainment – including its end! – and a natural way of lessening the intensity of alcohol-fuelled conversation with those around you. You don't get locked in a corner by one person when you are sitting around a table.

I have had some brilliant evenings out in my new found sobriety with all my old drinking friends. And I never fail to feel amazing when I flop into bed and awake with a clear head and no anxiety the next morning!

Have They Stopped Wanting to See Me?

Well, it's hard to be sure. I haven't noticed a radical difference. I've had fewer invitations to things from some quarters, and occasionally I feel that I'm putting heavy drinkers on their best behaviour when I'm around. I can almost sense the exhalation when I announce that it's time for me to go. That's not to say my presence isn't welcome, but I know when a social occasion moves towards "let-your-hair-down" time, and I used to love it when that happened. I'm no longer in that gang, and I'm relieved for it. I spent a lot of time there in the past.

What do I do with my time?

When I gave up alcohol, I thought I would have so much more time and energy on my hands and that I would get tons of stuff done as a result.

In reality, I haven't noticed a great difference. I feel tired and ready for bed by 10 p.m. Though I get up earlier than I used to, I don't always use that time particularly productively. I do enjoy it though, and for that alone I'm hugely grateful.

I still make lists that I don't complete, I exercise more, and I keep things in a more orderly state. But these things all take time in themselves, so I don't feel I have hours on my hands to fill. Quite the contrary.

I'm learning to appreciate my time, and realising that it doesn't need to be filled. I need to cherish and enjoy every moment, however uneventful. Alcohol demands that we crank everything up. I don't need to do that. I shouldn't try to live like that because it sets unrealistic expectations.

How Does It Feel Looking at Other People Drinking?

For the first six months after quitting alcohol, I

noticed anyone drinking from a can or bottle on the street and found that for a split second, and only that, it nearly always made me envious. I had to at least glance to see if the can was an alcohol brand. Oddly, if it wasn't, I was always slightly disappointed. For some strange reason, I found that whilst I could go past pubs without too much thought of diving inside them to get drunk in a dark corner, if I saw an old building that was once a Victorian pub in former years, it made me feel melancholic for the good old days.

Such pubs were symbols of my former self. We had all given up the booze and were carrying on in our new re-branded existence. I would gaze upon such buildings conspiratorially and fondly and try to imagine the dramas they housed. I would hanker for the good old days, whether my own or the Victorian ones of yesteryear.

In company, I drank vicariously through my friends. I wanted them to drink heavily so that I could witness the effects, either good or bad, and it helped me to appreciate my sobriety all the more. The only pangs I suffered were at the beginning of the evening when the first drinks were offered, poured, and devoured. But as I would always have had a few drinks before going out, such pangs were somewhat misplaced anyway. Besides, they faded away quickly.

After my first year of sobriety, I stopped noticing other people's drinking on these social occasions.

I was aware it was happening and noting who was doing what but only in passing, and without temptation or disappointment.

I was at a celebratory dinner the other day, sitting next to a couple, neither of whom I had met before. I began to feel so much compassion for Keith, the drinker in the relationship, as he grabbed the last bottle on the table with both hands in self-mocking desperation and poured the half glass that it contained. Tricia, his partner, was apologising for Keith's behaviour, but when someone suggested opening another bottle, he almost cried with delight and relief, oblivious to Tricia's protestations. He was beyond caring what people thought of his drinking.

He wasn't going to benefit from any more wine, but he didn't care about that. His conversation, level of concentration, and self-awareness were all on the downward path, and I pitied Keith for it. How many times did he find himself in this place? Maybe not every night, or even every week, in which case he would have looked forward to this moment as a chance to let his hair down. He would have got the evening out of proportion and the following day forgotten much of the detail. Maybe he would have stayed off alcohol for days or weeks until the next time, when he would binge again. He might have elected not to socialise for a while, demonstrate to Tricia, and to himself that he wasn't, isn't, dependent on alcohol. Besides, for Keith, just as for my former self, socialising isn't the same without alcohol. So, why bother with it if you can't drink?

I remembered all the feelings that Keith so clearly was experiencing. I had experienced them myself maybe a thousand times before. And at this celebratory dinner, almost two years sober, I was having a great time chatting and joking with a mixture of old and new friends. I felt relaxed and entertained, and at the end of the night, I drove Jane home and the next morning I went for a run in the early morning. I felt fantastic. And yes, a little too pleased with myself, I'm afraid to admit.

Christmas and Other Big Festivals – Glastonbury!

You can never predict how you are going to feel, even at the most ritualistically alcoholic events in your life.

Glastonbury Festival was, and is, an annual event for me, and my first without alcohol came around just six months into sobriety. I really didn't know quite how I would feel exactly, but I was very excited because this was such a great opportunity to find other sources of amusement to alcohol. If boredom crept in, then there was always something new to try out. But I knew it was a risky test. However, in the end, the whole experience was altered by the fact that I was coming down with bronchitis. I felt ill throughout the festival. Being without alcohol wasn't going to be problem for me after all, as I had other things on my mind. In fact, it took months to shrug off the infection. When at last I felt fit again, I was by then 10 months sober, and Christmas was around the corner – the other big ritualistic drinking event.

Now Christmas was far harder than I expected. I thought that after so many months alcohol-free I was fine, that I could enjoy myself in the company of drinkers on my special new drug called sobriety, but I just found the whole thing completely flat. Christmas shopping was…well, just shopping. I had been used to dropping into new and old-favourite pubs for some festive grog and a chat with a bartender to keep me going – savour the moment, keep it all jolly. Then meet up with a friend for some more drinks. I loved Christmas. I got into the festive mood instantly with a whisky Mac inside me, and I had the perfect excuse to have one at any moment of the day or night, for a whole month.

Suddenly, not having the booze left me unsure of what it was I liked about this time of year. Was it just the booze? What could I now look forward to? All those rituals, characterised by the drink best associated with them – ginger wine with guests, brandy on the pudding and in the pies, mulled wine when it's cold, red wine with pre-Christmas meals. Eggnog? (Non-drinking households all boast a bottle of eggnog which their owners think is very funny. They laboriously search the cupboard where it sits and produce the dusty bottle, making certain that everyone can see just how funny they find it.

That's because it's a badge that ironically conveys their non-drinking self-satisfaction. I always said yes and drank as much of it as possible since it's such a joke. God, they pissed me off!)

In my new, sober world, the prospect of decorating the tree, once a great excuse for all the festive drinks I could openly drink as well as sneak, had lost its appeal and I was unprepared for the disappointment. Then there were the three main days of Christmas itself, spent with my elderly parents, and which normally would have been a time to do nothing much but chat and drink. Now, in the new world, it was just chat. Something was missing, and I felt it. If I was bored, no longer could I just open a bottle of red wine to amuse myself.

But I had survived a year, and as I approached my sobriety anniversary, I felt as if a weight had lifted. I was already feeling in good shape mentally and physically. Spiritually, I felt calmer than ever before and better focused on the here and now than I ever thought possible. In the old days, I relied entirely on booze. It did all the work. Now, I had to work out what I wanted to do – for myself. I couldn't let alcohol tell me what I wanted.

My sobriety started to influence my outlook on life in even more positive ways. I didn't see money as the means to drinking opportunities anymore. In my drinking days, every penny earned was allocated to activities involving alcohol, either in a bar or an airport or aeroplane, a restaurant, a pub, on holiday, at a match, after a show. All fantasies about the lottery involved booze. My life was logistically organised around great drinking opportunities. It started with social occasions and gradually over the years it spread everywhere else. If I wasn't actually doing it, I was planning or at least thinking about drinking – or worrying about it. It never went away.

Airports... and Holidays

During the first six months of sobriety, Jane and I went to Rome for a few days.

I noted the differences at every turn to my drinking days. The airport, of course. I peered in to see if anyone was drinking pints in the departure lounge bars at 7am. I felt strangely reassured to see that they were. I wanted at least a few people to be carrying on the way I used to. I didn't want to join them, but I couldn't bear to see the opportunity go by completely wasted. I made use of my three core principles several times in the departure lounge at Gatwick, and I was glad not to have to make a decision whether to have a drink or not.

In the streets of Rome, I noticed bars and restaurants and their glasses and bottles of familiar drinks on every table. At 6pm., I had a pang and a feeling of deflation as aperitif time came and went. I wanted to drink vicariously through Jane, and when she said no to a second glass of wine, I felt frustrated at her abstemiousness. She was allowed to drink and yet wasn't taking advantage – on holiday! I loved the food and was able to relish every course and every mouthful. No longer was I using the food as an excuse for drinking, worrying if another bottle of wine could be ordered, and I could enjoy the coffee without having to think of it as an interference with alcohol. I ordered sparkling water with wild abandon and felt supremely cool and in control when I did. My sweet tooth (I never thought I had one) was coming through fast and strong too, and I was only too delighted to indulge it to the maximum. I had energy for exercise too and ran every morning along the banks of the Tiber in rain or sunlight, and I felt alive and free, empowered, and completely re-invented.

Nowadays, I take the view that if everything around me feels dull, that's because it probably is. Do something fun if you feel bored. Drinking doesn't need to be the centre of any activity anyway.

Airports… and holidays: One Year In

So, in this new freedom, entering my second year of sobriety, Jane and I went to Lisbon for a short break.

It was by then 14 months after I stopped drinking. It was a whole new experience even from the Rome trip of the previous year. I hadn't realised how much my attitude towards alcohol had changed in the last 12 months. I no longer felt any anxiety around alcohol. Unlike in Rome a year earlier, I no longer was peering in bars and restaurants or thinking about the days when I might have engineered the itinerary towards such a place where we would stay for hours on end – all day if possible. I didn't notice the bar at Gatwick on the way out to Lisbon, and the thought of alcohol never crossed my mind before the flight – the first time in my adult life. A city break would always have centred around alcohol. So, to be visiting a capital city in winter, when there is little else to do but sight-see around the capital, it's a miracle that I was able to do this without pangs for the old days. I would never have believed this was possible, let alone enjoyable.

How would I react if something terrible happened? Would I hit the bottle?

The strangest part about my sobriety has been how easily my head has been turned, albeit momentarily, by insignificant temptations, like an open bottle of brandy on the kitchen counter, or someone drinking a can of beer on the street. On such occasions I have had the impulse to drink. By contrast, much bigger, more obvious temptations like celebratory parties, or emotional traumas, I haven't had any such yearnings for alcohol at all.

Until it happened, my response to disaster and whether I would be tempted to hit the bottle, was one of the big unknowns.

Then my mum had a couple of falls. I had raced over to her flat in time to go with her in the ambulance to the hospital. It was all very scary, but under control, and I felt reassured by the care she was receiving. She seemed comfortable and content. I thought she would be in hospital for a short while and then we'd have to sort out when she would be able to come home or whether she would need be admitted to a dreaded care home. I wanted to avoid this if at all possible. It would feel like the end. I knew she had a long life still to live, and I wanted that life to be back at her flat. I was determined she got herself mobile again as soon as possible with any help the hospital could offer.

But she had so little energy. Every time I turned up at the ward, she would be asleep in her hospital bed. Nobody was able to tell me what was wrong with her. She had been put on painkillers so I was told, ready for the physiotherapist's and the occupational therapist's interventions. These pain killers were supposed to account for her grogginess. But she was also confused and very tired and seemed to be getting weaker all the time.

I had left her alone and gone home when she hadn't the energy to chat. I had escaped the intensity of the ward, guilt at my back, into the spring sunlight through the revolving doors of the hospital, and there it was: the pub. Only a split second was needed to turn towards the door, and I could have enjoyed the warm comfort of a glass of wine within moments. I didn't want it. I wanted to be in control of my situation and my emotions. I was back at Mum's bedside the next day, and the one after, and she just slept.

I sat by her bedside as they took her monitoring machines away. I tried to make bright conversation not knowing if she could hear me but knowing that this would be the last time I would speak to her. I wrote a list of our cherished memories over the years and read them to her. I thought of how irritable I had been with her in recent months when she had been stubborn, and I desperately wanted to somehow infiltrate her dream and say sorry and tell her she was right all along, absolutely right, and that I loved her.

When she died, I didn't really think about drinking. I don't know why I didn't. I had responsibilities to take care of. Maybe that was why. Mum and I had often reminded ourselves of a funny but apposite line in the film Clockwise: "The despair I can cope with… it's the hope." Now, here we were. No more hope left for Mum. I just had to get on with it, and wine wasn't going to help with that. It certainly wouldn't bring Mum back. I wanted to write a eulogy for her funeral, which a drink would only serve to ruin. I channelled all my heart into the eulogy, and it got me through the worst hours.

As tragic as Mum's death was for me, it didn't fill me with self-loathing. It didn't make me want to self-destruct. I wanted to be strong and come to terms with my feelings of loss. Alcohol might help me to wallow and cry uncontrollably, which I wasn't able to do, but I didn't want to be out of control ever again. So, it just wasn't a temptation to me.

What does a bad day feel like now?

Undeniably, there have been rough patches. I used a diary to record my feelings and here's part of an entry at 15 month's sober:

"Everything has felt peculiar today. I've had a sickly headache which the painkillers haven't penetrated, although they have had the effect of spreading the nauseous ache across my brain instead of in one isolated patch. I feel strangely emotional; like I'm going to burst into tears. I have felt drained of energy and I can't be bothered with anything, but not so as that I get tetchy with things, I just don't care about them. Tiredness has never had that effect. In the past it's always made me irritable and shouty. It's the nearest feeling to a hangover I've had in a year and three months of sobriety.

I would only ever associate this kind of feeling with the after-effects of booze, but the comparison isn't appropriate, as I've never had this exact feeling before. It's the emotional bit I'm finding strangest. I'm lost. Maybe it's that I have been flat-lining for so long, the spike in this emotional low has taken me off-guard?"

Irritation could strike and still does at any time though. I can go several hours at a stretch feeling intensely irritable. It feels as if objects are ganging up against me, hiding in places where I won't see them; people walk into me as I negotiate the pavement on foot; cars swing around every corner I am about to cross. I feel like shouting and howling and bursting into tears. Then, the mood passes. Gone in an instant; I can suddenly feel calm and content again.

Today, I still have an addictive attitude. I crave coffee and wait for it to lift me almost spiritually as I take the first sips from the cup. Sometimes it doesn't happen and I feel the disappointment or sometimes that coffee has to be joined by a chocolate brownie and the moment has to be just right, and I mustn't rush it and spoil the effect. I try to recreate the feeling of when it was amazing. It doesn't always work as I guzzle the coffee and scoff the brownie and don't savour the moment, and then it's all gone, and I haven't had the hit I craved so much. But do I buy 11 more brownies and 14 more coffees? No, I don't.

Highs and Lows

The strange thing is that in many ways life itself is much the same as it was before I quit drinking. The highs aren't quite as high and the lows not as low, but I still look forward and enjoy a special meal out on the weekend or a BBQ with friends or a trip to the theatre and even an evening in the pub.

I don't have the same expectations and excitement anymore, but I still have a good time, and at the end of the evening, I enjoy getting home – and I love waking the next day. I don't get a terrible low feeling after an event.

Mornings are my greatest joy, in fact, because the contrast is still so enormous in comparison with my former life. The optimism each day brings is truly wonderful.

Social occasions are still fun but never wild or unpredictable in the way they once were. I can't say that's a bad thing though. I no longer want to pay the price of that wildness and unpredictability – which is very high when it all goes wrong. Besides, I've done all that already, it's time to move on and try something new.

I realise now what a relief it is not to be thinking about alcohol all the time. It filled my every planning moment. I would have thought many times in the day whether I wanted a drink, and if so, whether I would actually have one. If I did have one, I'd be thinking about having the next one and how many more I'd need to have to keep chasing the buzz.

Now, I have the freedom to think about other things uninterrupted by thoughts of drinking.

Whilst the emotional flat-lining can on occasion be disappointing compared with the rollercoaster days, the level of alertness I possess at all times is itself exciting. I can wake in the night quickly if necessary, and certainly an early morning start is a joy, especially if there is something enjoyable to wake early for. Daytime fatigue is no longer caused by booze, but by "natural" causes.

I am now able to live my life in the present for the first time. What I do on a daily basis is what I want to be doing – now. It's not always exciting, but the contentment is everything. It's what I not only need but want. I never in my wildest dreams thought I would be able to enjoy that level of equilibrium.

My continued attendance at AA has been to remind myself of what an amazing thing I have done, in case I take it for granted. I know that if the day comes when I just don't care about sobriety anymore, I will drink. Not even because I want to, but self-destruction is not beyond me, I know that. AA reminds me of what a curse drinking is for people in desperation, and I need to be reminded, just in case.

I thought my bad moods were all caused by alcohol. They weren't. I have a short temper and an irrational belief that luck is against me. I think I turned to alcohol to run away from these feelings in the past, without realising until now that it fuels what is already there. It's how alcohol deceives us on many levels.

I am learning to relax in company. I always thought I needed alcohol. When I stopped drinking, I had to pick up from where I was, age 14. I had let alcohol shield me from nerves and social embarrassment. But therefore I hadn't learned how to deal with those things sober. I seem to be getting better at those things now and quite relish social functions where I can practice my new skills.

I don't miss the sense of panic that takes hold when alcohol is not available at a social function, or only limited amounts, after I had already given myself the green light to drink.

I don't miss the feeling of the party coming to an end and the depression that follows for days or the self-loathing if I played the goat or got into a disagreement and can't remember all the details. The need to drink again to feel better about myself.

I don't miss being drunk in a field for a week at a festival, covered in mud and ready for a sharpener from the moment I awoke. Nor do I miss all those theatre and cinema outings where the most important part was the drinks beforehand, during, and after the show.

I know that my relationship with alcohol is a power struggle that I am destined to lose if I drink. It's not so much the quantity I might drink or the trouble I might get into or the fun I might have. It's that I don't have any idea when I might want to stop once I've started. Circumstances won't always influence my desire for alcohol. So, the consequences can be terrible. Alcohol is far more powerful than I am.

I love a social occasion now. Nice food, fizzy drinks, and lovely coffee. Lots of people to talk to and a drive home to crawl into bed with my lovely partner and a good book. There is something so special in its ordinariness. It doesn't have to be a roller coaster. Now, the equilibrium is absolutely desirable.

Alcohol is a beautiful, shiny, inviting, exciting mirage, and if you aren't careful it will fool you as it fucks with your head, your heart, and your wallet.

Financial consequences

Since giving up alcohol, I have stopped haemorrhaging money. I spend a fraction of what I did. Restaurant bills are halved, the theatre is just the price of the ticket, so too is the cinema. I don't take taxis anywhere and rarely buy take-aways. Friends won't ever let me buy more than one drink for them, and at meals, I am not allowed to contribute to the alcohol bill.

I take money out at the cash point and it's still in my pocket, untouched two days later. My bank balance is always better than expected.

I am able to budget. I know how much a night out will cost me and can set parameters on what I want to spend. It makes a big difference not having to buy multiple bottles of wine just because others aren't keeping pace with my drinking.

When I first got sober, the thought of having nothing to spend my money on was deflating, like finding a trunk full of £50 notes on a desert island. Now, I just feel freedom even from the need for money as well as alcohol. Sure, I need to work, but it's a different need. I can take extended breaks. I can take less well-paid jobs on short-term contracts and walk away when they are done. I'm not funding my alcohol habit anymore.

For the record, I have lost over two stone in weight, I have come off blood-pressure medication, I run five days a week, and if needed I can function on as little as four hours sleep.

I wake feeling great, the novelty of which never wears off, not even slightly.

What Does My Future Hold?

Can I see myself staying sober for the rest of my life? According to AA, you shouldn't ask questions like that. The buzz-term in AA is – Just for Today. Oddly, I don't find much comfort in that phrase. I understand the sentiment well enough. If you think you'll never have a drink again, you may succumb to the enormity of it all and start drinking. But if you take it one day at a time, that's a small enough stretch to get your head around.

I felt diametrically opposed to this kind of thinking from the start. If it's just for today, then why bother? What's a day going to do in the big scheme of things. I always wanted to see the big picture and know that each day was another segment completed in the grand whole. I needed a bigger goal than one day to make it all worthwhile. Sure it would be harder at the start, but that's true of almost everything in life. If it's worth having, you need to work at it. The difficulty was in seeing that it was worth having. Once I had understood that, then I was more than prepared to work at it.

What Lessons Can Be Learned From My Own Experience?

I have attempted to answer that question in the final two chapters of this book.
The first lesson concerns the significance of the alcoholic question – if I know I'm not an alcoholic, should that affect what I do about my drinking? Is it important to establish 'how' alcoholic I really am? I will attempt to provide an answer to that question in relation to my own case and go on to suggest its significance, generally, to the quitting process.

The second is about desire. I urge the reader to take a step back and philosophically consider the importance that desire for alcohol plays in their continued drinking and whether they are interested in challenging that desire by putting it under the spotlight.

If I asked you now, do you *want* to stop drinking, you may very well answer *No*. And if you don't Want to stop drinking, then you probably won't. Desire is crucial in determining what you decide to do. But if I asked you if you were willing to put that desire to the test, to see how well it stands up to your own scrutiny, you might agree to give it a try.

Of course, it's perfectly possible that your desire for alcohol will be unaffected by the scrutiny I suggest. That's fine. At least you know this book is here to help at a later date, should alcohol cause you problems in the future. You might find your desire for it isn't invincible after all.

I hope you are willing to try!

CHAPTER FOUR

Am I an Alcoholic?

I never thought of myself as alcoholic. I'm told it's in the nature of the disease that alcoholics don't see themselves as such. This is a circular argument of course, but I can see the truth in it nonetheless. My latest increase in consumption was always the result of something that justified it – a tricky patch at work, a family argument, a love-interest that died. I would excuse the spike in my drinking based on whatever the special circumstances surrounding it were, convincing myself that once things were back to normal, so would my level of drinking – and that is apparently an alcoholic way of thinking.

I can accept that this refusal to admit I might have a problem is a necessary condition of alcoholism. But surely it's not a sufficient condition?

Where I'm less willing to concede to the alcoholic

diagnosis is where it concerns the level of control I had on my intake. AA members talk a great deal about their former lack of control over alcohol. Indeed, they talk about the powerlessness they used to have over it. The very first step of the 12 step tradition in AA is an admission of the powerlessness over alcohol, the admission that one's life has become unmanageable.

I didn't drink to blackout every time I drank. I rarely drove a car with alcohol inside me, and I never drove when over the limit. I didn't drink if I had to take command of a situation – such as a job interview, or a presentation. I was quite capable of staying sober until it was clear to drink.

I felt that I had control over my drinking. Yes, I did things that might seem alcoholic to an outsider – like drinking vodka on the streets and on the London Underground – sometimes on the way to work in the morning – but only on occasions when I had sanctioned such behaviour in the cold light of sobriety. They were never occasions where my drinking involved risk-taking, where I could be found out. They were only ever on slow days when nothing was happening.

The proof of that statement lay in the fact that nobody ever challenged me about my behaviour on these occasions. I never 'let myself go' after drinking in these circumstances. I always hid what I was doing, and its effects, from public suspicion.

Of course I got a bit out of control in social drinking situations – all drinkers do that. I was no saint, for sure. But in public I wasn't particularly worse or better than any of the drinkers I knew.

Perhaps most importantly of all, my drinking wasn't driven by a physical dependence. I didn't pour cider into me in order to stop a shaking hand. I certainly didn't drink mouth-wash or Meth's when alcohol was absent.

And funnily enough, even now, in sobriety, I still feel that my perceived level of control counted for something. It meant I wasn't as bad as others. It meant that if I was alcoholic then there must be a scale, and that I was at the lower end of it.

Writing this book made me realise that in trying to understand how and why I had stopped drinking I had been asking the wrong questions. Questions like "Am I an alcoholic?" or "Do I drink too much?" are always going to lead to an endless round of self-justification.

For me, the key was to look at my relationship with alcohol away from the question of units consumed, blackouts, drinking alone, and dry Januaries. What suddenly worked for me was a different question entirely.

I found myself asking "What is alcohol still doing for me?" It was all about bringing my drinking into sharp focus – putting it in the dock for cross examination, asking it what it was continuing to offer.

I started to question why the buzz didn't last all night and sometimes didn't come at all – I questioned why it put me in a sarcastic and hateful mood sometimes, without warning – I questioned why I found myself drinking more and more of it when I knew it was better not to – asking why I planned so much of my activity to please it, while ignoring everything else – asking why I always thought it would make me feel better when so often it made me feel worse the next day – filled with remorse and anxiety.
It was from these questions that I was able to see for the first time that not drinking was a brilliant solution to a whole range of problems.

The desire for sobriety grew very fast indeed from then on.

It was when I questioned alcohol's key attractions that I realised how tired I had become of its effect on my brain and behaviour. I then just needed to focus on a whole new adventure into something completely unknown.

I was lucky that circumstances brought about this cross-examination of the benefits of alcohol. Without the dilemma I found myself in I probably wouldn't have brought my desire for alcohol into question. There would have been no need. The solution to my dilemma would probably have been to opt for a dry January and then go back to drinking at the end of it.

The only thing I knew for sure was that I didn't want to go through all of it again and that taking a drink now would guarantee I'd have to.

The only requirement for membership to AA is "a desire to stop drinking," and that was what I suddenly had.

AA became my protection from myself – in case I decided it was okay to have a drink. AA reminded me of what an amazing thing it is to be sober.

Up until this point, drinking was the prop that got me through life, and I didn't stop to contemplate life without it, because life without it was unimaginable. I might from time to time consider if I was maybe drinking too much of it, and I only asked that question out of fear – the fear that I might have to stop drinking if I found that I was.

But where drinking is concerned, you only find what you want to believe. If AA is right, you'll go on believing you don't have a problem until alcohol has pinned you into a corner. I now understand their claim (AA's core belief) that you have to hit rock-bottom in order to turn your life around. Because until you hit rock bottom, you will always look for, and find, an excuse for your drinking. You will always believe in your own ability to get a grip once the storm has passed. You will always kick the can down the road.

If pressed for an answer about my alcoholism, I would say I was psychologically but not physically dependent; that I was a functioning alcoholic not an abusive alcoholic and that I could have carried on setting rules around my own drinking for some time to come, albeit with unpredictable levels of success. However, if Jane had eventually left me, I might have decided to stop drinking and win her back, or if that didn't work, I might have increased my drinking and thereby taken a step closer to a life of unmanageability that AA talks so much about.

I suspect I was like millions of people, for whom this book is aimed at, people who are just about able to keep a lid on their drinking, but who nonetheless are ruled by it – making plans around it, trying not to drink too much of it, trying to get enough of it, sacrificing almost everything for it. And like millions of people I was vulnerable in times of stress when my intake might rise sharply.

Whether I am alcoholic or not seems to me to be relatively unimportant. It was my relationship with alcohol that was the problem. I had come to rely on it too much in social settings, at first for confidence, then later for entertainment, and it had stunted my emotional growth. It had also shrunk my ambition, being ready to console at every moment when things didn't go quite right. And it had sapped me of energy and of money.

In the end, I wanted it whenever it felt safe to have it, and I moved heaven and earth to pave the way for it at all possible occasions, and if I couldn't have it, I was tetchy and irritable. I was on the wrong path and now I wanted to get onto a new one before it was too late. I wanted to grow up and start finding out more about myself which meant going back and picking up a journey I shirked when I was 14. I think there's just enough time to do that now, but I have left it quite late.

CHAPTER FIVE

Desire – and the Resistance to Change

Looking back on my life and into my very soul to see what made me, me, I can see that at the heart was the belief that alcohol was the magic ingredient to any given situation.

Other than playing sports or driving a car, I couldn't imagine any activity that wouldn't be made either more enjoyable or more bearable with alcohol.

So, when I finally put down the drink, I struggled to understand how and why I was able to just stop in the way that I did. My mother had done a similar thing after 25 years of hell. One day, the desire for alcohol wasn't there anymore.

What I am interested to know is: can this sudden change of desire be self-motivated?

Strictly speaking the answer to that must be No.

To address your desire for unwanted things, you have to un-want them.

But you can get around this by focussing on your desire for alcohol and asking questions of it that you may not have considered before.

While you are drinking, ask yourself what mental state alcohol is evoking and why that feels desirable? Ask yourself if you are feeling a buzz from alcohol and how long that buzz is lasting? Ask if you are able to get that buzz going again after it has subsided, and if not, why you are carrying on drinking? If you think the next drink will start to have a noticeable effect on you, like a slur, focus on whether you really want that noticeable effect, and if you don't want it, ask yourself why you are carrying on anyway?

You need to try and defend your continued drinking with actual answers to these questions in your head, even if they sound ridiculous to you. You need to try and rationalise what you are doing so that you can examine your habit in a new light, recalling the answers you gave to your questions. It may well be that you can't think of a reason why you carry on drinking when the buzz has gone, only that you just can't stop drinking once you've started. This is still useful as it helps you to understand why you carry on drinking the way you do. By getting to a deeper understanding of what you are doing and why, you have a greater chance of changing your desires.

Before you have that first drink, focus on what you hope it will do for you – just the first one. If you know it will lead on to many more, ask yourself if you have already done the drinking thing a thousand times before and is it not rather predictable? Could you be ready to shun that first drink and try something different – is it time for a change? If you can bring your desire for the first drink into question, then it's even easier to bring all the others into question too. By focussing hard on each mouthful of alcohol, you may find that each one does very little more than the last one, and you might conclude in the end that it's not as desirable as you thought it was.

If you are worried about your high level of drinking, don't look around you and seek reassurance in that terrible white elephant, that others drink more than you, or that I, the author of this book, was a heavier drinker than you are now. Don't assume that just because you have a job and a steady hand in the morning, that you have nothing to worry about, yet. Open your mind. Challenge the assumptions you always make about alcohol and its benefits. Don't try to protect it at all costs. Analyse your habit, evaluate each drink over a period of time.

With a different attitude to alcohol, you stand a chance of changing your desire for it. That is the aim.

Desire is the key to success. It's no different from smoking or gambling in that respect. Unless you want to stop, you probably won't.

To un-want alcohol or sugar or caffeine or cocaine is 50% of the battle. Perhaps more than 50%. The method you choose for the remainder of the battle is much easier. Take your pick: acupuncture, counselling, self-help, group therapy, hypnosis – they all work if the desire is there.

I wrote in the preface to *Not Alcoholic, But...* that this book was especially for all those drinkers who from time to time worry if they might have a problem with alcohol. That is because 'worry' is a potential motivator for change and might have been your inspiration for reading this book. If so, instead of focusing purely on alcohol consumption, dry months, cutting down, and the definitions of alcoholism, I urge the concerned drinker to focus on their relationship with alcohol. Ask the questions I have listed above.

If your desire for alcohol is unshaken by this cross-examination, then so be it. Perhaps you are not ready for a change. What I hope I have offered in this book is the chance to see for yourself if you are ready. If not, you can come back to the questions at another time – or you can come up with a whole different set of questions of your own, tailored to your individual alcoholic tastes. But I hope this book has got you thinking about alcohol in a different way – enough to allow a change, if that's what you decide you would like.

For me, a change of desire was initiated by circumstances – a fall from grace and an ill-timed party forced me to look for new solutions to my problem – and in that short time, I allowed some doubt about alcohol to creep in.

Why did I never question my desire before that? I think it's because for most of my life I didn't want to imagine a world without alcohol. I didn't want to question alcohol's ability to help me enjoy or endure life. Whether I could survive without alcohol wasn't the issue, it was all about happiness. I just couldn't imagine being happy without alcohol. But I never dared test if that were really true, and so I drank for 36 years.

Alcohol will always let me down in the end; unpredictably of course, laughing with me one moment, then spinning round and head-butting me in the face the next.

For that reason, I have no desire to invite it back into my life - ever again.

APPENDIX

Measuring Your Relationship with Alcohol

National guidelines tell us what the safe limits of alcohol are. It was 21 units per week for a man when I started writing this book and 14 for a woman. Now, they have been brought in line with each other to the lower level of 14. They are bound to change again before long. It doesn't make much difference. To a drinker, they hardly register on the weekly total, but I seem to remember being relieved whenever I read about a new piece of research that suggested a higher number of weekly units was safe.

Whilst I don't wish to challenge the validity of the guidelines, I do think they fall short when it comes to giving practical advice to drinkers because they don't give a complete picture.

By that I mean, I could have been drinking within the above guidelines, but sitting on an unexploded bomb.

I have developed a more comprehensive measurement tool to focus on my relationship with alcohol.

It centres on three variables: consumption, desire (for alcohol) and restraint. The national guidelines focus only on the first, and admittedly the other two are not strictly speaking quantifiable, so honesty is vital.

I picked out a number of social occasions from my drinking days and applied my evaluation method retrospectively to each one. The less boozy the occasion, the more telling the results.

I gave myself a score for the consumption of alcohol, 10 being for the biggest quantity. Then I gave myself an overall score for the level of desire I felt to drink on that occasion and also a score for the amount of restraint I used, if any, to drink the quantity I did.

A score of 15 or above meant there was a problem in my relationship with alcohol on a given occasion (in my estimation).

Example 1

A boozy night out where I intended and wanted to have plenty to drink looked like this:
Consumption: 8
Desire: 8

Restraint: 2

Total score: 18
Much of my drinking was like this.

Example 2

An occasion at which I wanted to drink freely but had already pledged to hold back.

Consumption: 2
Desire: 8
Restraint: 8

Although I had kept within the national guidelines, I had to restrain my desire for alcohol. So, desire and restraint score highly. I believe that desire and restraint are every bit as important as consumption in measuring my relationship with alcohol.

Example 3

An occasion at which I was out celebrating with some boozy friends but was not in the mood for heavy drinking. I knew I had to drink in rounds, and it would be expected of me to keep up at the same pace as everyone else.

Consumption: 8
Desire: 3
Restraint: 1

You can see how the problem in Example 3 is rather different from your problem in Example 1 even though the level of consumption is the same. In this example, if I wanted to do something about my consumption, it would be a question of altering my social arrangements more than my psychological outlook, which is a different kind of problem.

Ideally, you want to get your drinking to a level where the consumption is at your own set limit – for which you might give yourself a score of 2.

Your restraint and desire are key to the next bit. If you are doing it right, your desire will be at 2 and so will your restraint, which will always be low if your desire is also low.

The official line you hear trotted out by those in authority is to get yourself away from places where heavy drinking is expected of you. That's great advice if your problem is only a social one. It doesn't help if your desire for alcohol is high because you'll just find somewhere else to drink.

Alternatively, you can set yourself some hard and fast rules, and these may work for you, enough to keep your consumption within safe levels. That's great too. But at what cost? Would you not be better off without the temptation?

There must be thousands of drinkers who have managed to keep their drinking in check over the years who secretly long to drink heavily every time alcohol is available, and perhaps every now and then, they get that opportunity – once a week at the book or golf club or every fortnight at the football or rugby match, or at Christmas and birthdays.

When I share my thoughts in AA meetings now, I tend to focus on self-restraint. I need to remind myself how miserable it was to have to hold back so much of the time. I got tired of needing to restrain my drinking, whether I achieved it or not on a given occasion.

To be free of that now is the most liberating feeling in the world, and one that I feel most keenly when bottles of wine are open on the table and everyone around me is having a good time. And that's because I'm having an even better one than everyone else!

Printed in Great Britain
by Amazon